D0249993

BUILDING RESTAURANT PROFITS

How to Ensure Maximum Results

By Jennifer Hudson Taylor & Douglas R. Brown

The Food Service Professional's Guide To:
Building Restaurant Profits
How to Ensure Maximum Results: 365 Secrets Revealed

Atlantic Publishing Group, Inc. Copyright © 2003
1210 SW 23rd Place
Ocala, Florida 34474
800-541-1336
352-622-5836 - Fax

www.atlantic-pub.com - Web Site
sales@atlantic-pub.com E-mail

SAN Number :268-1250

International Standard Book Number: 0-910627-19-3

Library of Congress Cataloging-in-Publication Data

Hudson Taylor, Jennifer.
Building restaurant profits : how to ensure maximum
results: 365 secrets revealed / by Jennifer Hudson Taylor.
 p. cm. -- (The food service professionals guide to ; 9)
Includes bibliographical references and index.
ISBN 0-910627-19-3 (pbk. : alk. paper)
1. Restaurants--Finance.   I. Title. II. Series.
TX911.3.F5H69 2003
647.95'068'1--dc21
2002011690

Printed in Canada

Book layout and design by Meg Buchner of Megadesign
www.mega-designs.com • e-mail: megadesn@mhtc.net

CONTENTS

9. MARKETING FOR PROFITABILITY

10. BEHIND THE SCENES

You'll find great tips on how to build your restaurant's profits.

INTRODUCTION

B*uilding Restaurant Profits* is designed as a quick reference manual to help you take quick and easy actions to maximize profits from your restaurant business.

You won't find complicated theories that require additional interpretations or lengthy explanations. What you will find are actual tips that produce profitable results, without consuming all your time in unnecessary research, or worse, experiences of painful trial, risk and error. This book lists company names and contact information with corresponding tips, where appropriate.

Building Restaurant Profits is efficiently organized, with easy-to-recognize subject headings and highlighted bullets that lead you directly to the answers that you need. Unnecessary descriptions are replaced with the basic facts. This book is no ordinary textbook. Instead, it offers you actionable strategies and tips that provide profitable results for today.

*Your business plan
is your road map.*

CHAPTER ONE

GETTING STARTED

Write a Great Business Plan – If You Haven't Already!

Don't skimp on the business plan. If you are operating now, it's not too late to write that plan; it will be the road map to your success. Don't just be in business, have a financial plan; your business plan is the road map. If possible, take your time at the planning stage of your business and write a well-constructed, detailed business plan. Failure to do so is one of the commonest causes of business failure. Make sure that your plan covers the following basic information:

- Projected startup costs
- Personnel
- Insurance
- Rent
- Depreciation
- Loan payments
- Advertising/Promotions
- Legal/Accounting
- Miscellaneous expenses
- Supplies
- Payroll expenses
- Salaries/Wages
- Utilities
- Marketing costs
- Inventory costs
- Training costs
- Projected Profit & Loss Statements

- Projected Balance Sheets
- Any other known facets of running your restaurant business
- Additional costs:
  - Outsourcing labor costs for construction
  - Maintenance
  - Web site creation
  - Additional online marketing expenses

- **Business profile.** Include a business profile explaining the business, the history, economic and industry trends, target audience and marketing concepts, including operational procedures.

- **Financial section.** The financial section of your business plan should include:
  - Loan applications you've filed
  - Capital equipment and supply list
  - Balance sheet
  - Breakeven analysis
  - Pro-forma income projections (profit and loss statement)
  - Pro-forma cash flow

- **The income statement and cash-flow projections** should include:
  - A 3-year summary
  - Detail by month for the first year
  - Detail by quarter for the second and third years

- **Check out Quick Plan Restaurant Plans** online at www.atlantic-pub.com.

Financial Analysis

In order to make profits, you need to plan for profits. Many restaurants offering great food, great atmosphere and great service still go out of business. The reason for this is that they fail to manage the financial aspects of the business. This means that poor cost-control management will be fatal to your business. Furthermore, good financial management is about interpreting financial statements and reports, not simply preparing them. A few distinctions need to be made in order to understand the language we are now using:

- **Financial accounting.** These figures are primarily for external groups to assess taxes, the status of your establishment, etc.

- **Managerial accounting.** These figures provide information to internal users that become the basis for managing day-to-day operations. This data is very specific, emphasizes departmental operations and uses non-financial data like customer counts, menu sales mix and labor hours. These internal reports break down revenues and expenses by department, day and meal period so they can be easily interpreted, and areas that need attention can be seen. Daily and weekly reports must be made and analyzed in order to determine emerging trends.

The Present Financial Status of the Food Service Industry

Presently, throughout the entire food service industry, operating expenses are up and income is down. After taxes and expenses, restaurants that make money, according to the National Restaurant Association, have bottom lines at 0.5-3 percent of sales. This tiny percentage is the difference between being profitable and going under. This drives home the importance of controlling your costs and understanding the numbers. A lot can be done to control costs and it begins with planning. Here are the basics:

- **Cost control is about numbers.** It is about collecting, organizing, interpreting and comparing the numbers that impact your bottom line. This is not a job that can be delegated, because these numbers are your controls. They are what tell you the real story of what's going on in your restaurant.

- **Understanding the bottom line.** Understanding this story and its implications on your bottom line comes only with constant review and the resulting familiarity with the relationships between these numbers and the workings of the business. This may seem like drudgery, but it is, in fact, your key to understanding the meaning behind your numbers. Once you have mastered the numbers, they'll tell you the story behind your labor productivity, portion control, purchase prices, marketing promotions, new menu items and competitive strategy. This knowledge will free you to run the best, most profitable operation you can.

- **Chances of getting your money back.** According to government statistics, a restaurant investor has a 1-in-20 chance of getting his money back in five years. Furthermore, the consensus of many successful restaurateurs is that 80 percent of the success of a restaurant is determined before it opens. This means you must prepare. And part of that preparation is integrating an ongoing profit planning and cost-control program into your business.

- **Cost controls.** This can be doubly important if you are fortunate enough to start out doing great business. This is because high profits can hide much inefficiency that will surely expose itself during times of low sales. Too many people become cost-control converts only after suffering losses. This is shortsighted. The primary purpose of cost controls is to maximize profits, not minimize losses. Controlling costs works - all the time - because it focuses on getting the most value from the least cost in every aspect of your operation. By keeping costs under control, you can charge less than the competition or make more money from charging the same price.

- **Spending controls.** These are huge operating freedoms and opportunities that are not afforded you if you don't know what you're spending and, therefore, can't control that spending. Furthermore, most of the waste that occurs in restaurants can't be detected by the naked eye. It takes records and reports, whose meanings you've mastered interpreting, to tell you the size of the inefficiencies that are taking place.

Profit planning and cost control are information-gathering tools.

CHAPTER TWO

PROFIT PLANNING AND COST CONTROL

This is not accounting or bookkeeping. Profit planning and cost control are the information-gathering tools. Profit planning and cost control can be defined by explaining their purposes:

- **To provide management with information** needed for making day-to-day operations decisions.

- **To monitor department and individual efficiency.**

- **To inform management of expenses** being incurred and incomes received and whether they fall within standards and budgets.

- **To prevent fraud and theft.**

- **To provide the groundwork for the business's goals** (not for discovering where it has been).

- **To emphasize prevention,** not correction.

- **To maximize profits,** not minimize losses.

- **The idea of prevention versus correction is fundamental.** Prevention occurs through advanced planning. Your primary job is not to put out fires, it's to prevent them - and to maximize profits in the process.

Cost-Control Records - Get It Right

The larger the distance between an owner or manager and the actual restaurant, the greater the need for effective cost-controls records. This is how franchisers of restaurant chains keep their eyes on thousands of units across the world. Many managers of individual operations assume that since they're on the premises during operating hours, a detailed system of cost control is unnecessary. Tiny family operations often see controls the same way and view any device for theft prevention as a sign of distrust towards their staff. This is short-sighted, because the main purpose of cost control is to provide information to management about daily operations. Prevention of theft is a secondary function. Cost controls are about knowing where you are going. Furthermore, most waste and inefficiencies cannot be seen; they need to be understood through the numbers:

- **Understanding those numbers means interpreting them.** To do this effectively, you need to understand the difference between control and reduction:

- **Control is achieved through the assembly and interpretation of data** and ratios on your revenue and expenses.

- **Reduction is the actual action taken to bring costs within your predetermined standards.** Effective cost control starts at the top of an organization. Management must establish, support and enforce its standards and procedures.

- **Take a look at the following sales and costs statistics:**

THE RESTAURANT SALES & COSTS SURVEY

	Full-Service Restaurant	Fast-Service Restaurant
Sales		
Food Sales	70-75%	90-95%
* Beverage Sales	30-25%	10-5%
Costs		
Cost of Food	26-36%	28-35%
* Cost of Beverages	10-22%	5-10%
Salaries - Labor	25-35%	25-35%
Employee Benefits	4-8%	4-8%
Occupancy Costs	3-8%	3-15%
Operating Costs - Other	1-20%	10-20%
Pre-Tax Income	3-6%	5-12%
Includes Liquor & Wine Sales & Costs		

Get Computerized

The reality is, no matter what type or size of your food service operation, our advice is get your operation computerized. It's extremely difficult to compete successfully without utilizing technology, at least to some degree. Today the investment for a basic computer and accounting software is less than $2,000 and could be as little as $1,000. The investment will deliver immediately in savings in accounting fees and your ability to get true insight into your business.

- **QuickBooks.** Our favorite restaurant accounting package is the veteran QuickBooks® by Intuit. The 2002 version of QuickBooks® is rich in features, including built-in remote-access capabilities and Web interfaces. Reports are generated in a few seconds that would take hours to calculate manually. The reports are also flawless, eliminating the human-error factor. This program now has a POS option that was the only limiting factor prior to this new release. The 2002 version of QuickBooks® is available at www.quickbooks.com. Another popular accounting package is Peachtree®, available at www.peachtree.com.

- **Tasty Profits software.** If you are just setting up your accounting program and decide to use QuickBooks®, we recommend an add-on product called "The Tasty Profits Guide to QuickBooks® Software for Restaurants." This helpful guide to QuickBooks® enables you to save thousands of dollars doing your own accounting with its proven, easy-to-use system. Simply install the floppy disc that is included with the "Tasty Profits Guide" directly into your computer. Download the pre-configured restaurant accounts, and you are ready to go. You will have instant access to all your financial data, calculate accurate food and bar costs with ease, reconcile bank and credit card statements, track and pay tips that are charged to credit cards and calculate sales tax automatically. The program costs about $70 and is available at www.atlantic-pub.com or 800-541-1336, Item TP-01.

Chart of Accounts

Restaurant accounting requires specific procedures. Concentrate on the essentials. The following suggestions will point you in the right direction:

- **The Uniform System of Accounts for Restaurants (USAR).** The National Restaurant Association publishes a simple, easy-to-use accounting classification system for restaurants. This valuable book, prepared by CPAs, includes examples of balance sheets, wage-control reports and an expense-classification system. If you take only one idea from this book, we recommend you use this system. You can order online at www.restaurant.org, or by calling 800- 424-5156. USAR is an essential guide for restaurant accounting. It establishes a common industry language that allows you to compare ratios and percentages across industry lines. The goal of this comparison is to create financial statements that are management tools, not just IRS reports.

- **The Operations Report.** The National Restaurant Association also publishes a report entitled "The Operations Report," based on an annual survey of operator income statements. Conducted jointly by the association and the accounting firm of Deloitte & Touche, the report provides detailed data on where the restaurant dollar comes from and where it goes, for four categories of restaurants: three types of full-service operations (with per-person check sizes under $10; between $10 and $25; and $25 and more) plus limited service (fast food operations).

- **Utilize the same chart of accounts to compare your operation with others.** Ratios enable you to compare the operating data of a specific hotel or restaurant to the average for a group of similar establishments. You may, for example, compare the assets of a particular restaurant with the average assets of restaurants of a similar size in order to determine if it is as financially healthy as it should be. You can easily compare food costs and other costs figures for comparisons.

Point-of-Sale Systems

The most widely used technology in the food service industry is the touch-screen, or point-of-sale (POS) system. The POS system is basically an offshoot of the electronic cash register. Touch-screen POS systems were introduced to the food service industry in the mid-1980s and have penetrated 90 percent of restaurants. nationwide. From fine-dining establishments to fast food, the touch-screen is effortless. In fact, a child could be trained to use it in a few minutes. Such systems will pay for themselves. According to information published by the National Restaurant Association, a restaurant averaging $1,000,000 in food-and-beverage sales can expect to see an estimated saving of $30,000 per year. Understanding the numbers collected by a POS system will give the operator more control over inventory, bar revenues, labor scheduling, overtime, customer traffic and service. Understanding POS data ultimately clarifies the bottom line, knocking guesswork out of the equation. Here is the lowdown:

- **A POS system comprises two parts:** the hardware, or equipment, and the software, the computer program that runs the system. This system allows waitstaff to key in their orders as soon as the customers give them. Additional keys are available for particular options and specifica-tions, such as "rare," "medium-rare" and "well-done." Some systems prompt the waitstaff to ask additional questions when the item is ordered, such as, "Would you like butter, sour cream or chives with the baked potato?" Some will suggest a side dish or a compatible wine.

- **Processing the order.** The order is sent through a cable to printers located throughout the restaurant: at the bar and in the kitchen and office. All orders must be printed before they are prepared, thus ensuring good control.

- **Payment.** When a server has completed the ordering, a guest check can be printed and later presented. Most POS systems allow certain discounts and require manager control over others. Charge cards, cash and checks can be processed separately and then reports can be generated by payment type.

Some benefits of using a POS system:
- Increases sales and accounting information.
- Customer tracking.
- Reports waitstaff's sales and performance.
- Reports menu-item performance.
- Reports inventory usage.
- Processes credit card purchases.
- Ensures accurate addition on guest checks
- Prevents incorrect items from being ordered.
- Prevents confusion in the kitchen.
- Reports possible theft of money and inventory.
- Records employee time-keeping.
- Reports menu-sales breakdown for preparation and menu forecasting.
- Reduces time spent walking to kitchen and bar.

- **POS enhancements.** Many POS systems have been greatly enhanced to include comprehensive home delivery, guest books, online reservations, frequent diner modules and fully integrated systems with real-time inventory, integrated caller ID, accounting, labor scheduling, payroll, menu analysis, purchasing and receiving, cash management and reports. Up-and-coming enhancements and add-ons include improved functionality across the Internet, centralized functionality enabling "alerts" to be issued to managers and voice-recognition POS technology.

- **The future.** As the labor market continues to diminish, touch-screens with POS systems will become essential. It has been predicted that in the next few years, customers may even place their own orders. Terminals will be simply turned around. During peak seasonal periods, ordering food may be like pumping your own gas; customers will key in their own selections and then slide their credit cards through to pay.

Crucial Elements of Cost Control – Profit Planning

There are ten primary areas that are central to any food and beverage operation and, therefore, are crucial elements of profit planning:

- **Purchasing.** Your inventory system is the critical component of purchasing. Before placing an order with a supplier, you need to know what you have on hand and how much will be used. Allow for a cushion of inventory so you won't run out between deliveries. Once purchasing has been standardized, the manager simply orders from your suppliers. Records show supplier, prices, unit of purchase, product specifications, etc. This information needs to be kept on paper and preferably computerized. Purchase food items according to usage. For example, if you plan to use tomatoes by blending and mixing them with other ingredients to make a sauce, then purchase broken tomatoes as opposed to whole tomatoes. However, if you intend to use tomatoes to decorate a dinner plate or as a topping, then opt for high-quality produce, such as baby plum vine-grown tomatoes.

- **Receiving.** This is how you verify that everything you ordered has arrived. Check for correct brands, grades, varieties, quantities, correct prices, etc. Incorrect receivables need to be noted and either returned or credited to your account. Products purchased by weight or count need to be checked.

- **Storage.** All food is stored until it's used. Doing so in an orderly fashion ensures easy inventory. Doing so properly, with regard to temperature, ventilation and freedom from contamination, ensures food products remain in optimum condition until being used. Expensive items need to be guarded from theft.

- **Issuing.** Procedures for removing inventory from storage are part of the cost-control process. Head chefs and bartenders have authority to take or "issue" stock from storage to the appropriate place. This is a much more important aspect of cost control than it seems, because in order to know your food and beverage costs you need to know your beginning inventory, how much was sold, and your ending inventory. Without this data, you can't determine accurate cost figures.

- **Rough preparation.** How your staff minimizes waste during the preliminary processing of inventory is critical.

- **Preparation for service.** Roughly prepared ingredients are finished off prior to plating. The quality and care with which this is done determines the amount of waste generated in preparation of standard recipes.

- **Portioning/transfer.** Food can be lost through over-portioning. Final preparation should be monitored regularly to ensure quality and quantity standards are being adhered to. This is such a crucial element to cost control that many managers are assigned to monitor order times, portions, presentation and food quality with an eagle eye.

- **Order taking/guest check.** Every item sold or issued from the kitchen needs to be recorded. This can be done by paper check or computer. Basically, it needs to be impossible for anyone to get food or drinks without the items being entered into the system. No verbal orders for food or beverages should be accepted by or from anybody - including management and owners.

- **Cash receipts.** Monitoring sales is crucial to cost controls. Under/overcharging, falsification of tips and lost checks must be investigated after every shift. Sales information from each meal period must be compiled to build a historical financial record. This record helps you forecast the future.

- **Bank deposits/accounts payable.** Proper auditing of bank deposits and charge slips must be conducted.

Accurate Day-to-Day Cost Control

Cost control is an ongoing process that must be part of the basic moment-to-moment breathing of your business. A continuous appraisal of this process is equally as integral to the functioning of your restaurant. Consider the following:

- **There are five key elements** to an effective cost-control strategy:
  - Planning in advance.
  - Procedures and devices that aid the control process.
  - Implementation of your profit-planning program.
  - Employee compliance.
  - Management's ongoing enforcement and reassessment.

- **Furthermore, your program should be assessed with the following questions:**
  - Do your cost controls provide relevant information?
  - Is the information timely?
  - Is it easily assembled, organized and interpreted?
  - Are the benefits and savings greater than the cost of the controls?

This last point is especially important. When the expense of the controls exceeds the savings, that's waste, not control. Spending $30,000 on an automated liquor dispensing system that will save you $5,000 in waste is ineffective.

Standards are Key to Any Cost Control Program

Predetermined points of comparison must be set, against which you will measure your actual results. The difference between planned resources and resources actually used are the variance. Management can then monitor for negative or positive variances between standards and actual performance and will know where specifically to make corrections. Here are the essential guidelines:

- **These five steps illustrate the uses of standards:**
  - Performance standards should be established for all individuals and departments.
  - Individuals must see it as the responsibility of each to prevent waste and inefficiency.
  - Adherence – or lack of adherence – to standards must be monitored.
  - Actual performance must be compared against established standards.
  - When deviations from standards are discovered, appropriate action must be taken.

- **Your job is to make sure standards are adhered to.** Is your staff using measuring scoops, ladles and sized bowls; glasses and cups; weighing portions individually; portioning by count and pre-portioning? These are all useful tools to make sure standards are met and your cost-control program is implemented effectively.

Cost Ratios

Owners and managers need to be on the same page in terms of the meaning and calculation of the many ratios used to analyze food, beverage and labor costs. It's important to understand how your ratios are being calculated so you can get a true indication of the cost or profit activity in your restaurant. Cost control is not just the calculation of these numbers; it's the interpretation of them and the appropriate (re)actions taken to bring your numbers within set standards. Consider the following:

- **Food-cost percentage.** This basic ratio is often misinterpreted because it is often calculated in so many different ways. Basically, it is food cost divided by food sales. However, whether your food cost is determined by food sold or consumed is a crucial difference. Also, for your food-cost percentage to be accurate, a month-end inventory must be taken. Without this figure, your food cost statement is inaccurate and, therefore, basically useless. This is because your inventory will vary month-to-month - even in the most stable environment (which yours probably won't be initially) - because months end on different days of the week.

- **Calculating inventory.** When conducting the ending or physical inventory, use scales for food and special scales for liquor for the most accurate determination. Place inventory sheets in the same order as the room is stocked. Use a separate sheet for each area. Include on the form: your inventory unit, units per case, pack or size, par and vendor code. Use two people, one to count (a manager) and one to record the figures (preferably an employee from a different area). For example, have the bar manager assist in the food inventory and the kitchen manager help in recording the liquor.

Cost Calculations - The Basics

Distinguishing between food sold and consumed is important. This is because all food consumed is not sold. Food consumed includes all food used, sold, wasted, stolen or given away to customers and employees. Food sold is determined by subtracting all food bought (at full price), from the total food consumed. Get to grips with the following:

- **Maximum allowable food-cost percentage (MFC).** This is the most food can cost and still return your profit goal. If at the end of the month your food-cost percentage is over your maximum allowable percentage, you won't meet your profit expectations. This is how you calculate it:
    - Write your dollar amounts of labor costs and overhead expenses and exclude food costs. Refer to past accounting periods and yearly averages to get realistic cost estimates.

    - Add your monthly profit goal as either a dollar amount or a percentage of sales.

    - Convert dollar values of expenses to percentages by dividing by food sales for the periods used for expenses. Generally, don't use your highest or lowest sales figures for calculating your operating expenses. Subtract the total of the percentages from 100 percent. The remainder is your maximum allowable food-cost percentage (MFC).

    - 100 - (monthly expenses – food costs) + monthly profit goal = MFC%

- **Actual food-cost percentage (AFC).** This is the percentage at which you're actually operating. It's calculated by dividing food cost by food sales (yes, only food sales, not total sales). If you are deducting employee meals from your income statement, then you are calculating cost of food sold. If there is no deduction of employee meals, which is true for most operations, then the food cost you're reading is food consumed. This is always a higher cost than food sold, and if inventory is not being taken, the food cost on your income statement is just an estimate based on purchases and isn't accurate.

- **Potential food-cost percentage (PFC).** This cost is sometimes called the theoretical food cost. PFC is the lowest your food cost can be, because it assumes that all food consumed is sold and that there is no waste whatsoever. Calculate this cost by multiplying the number sold of each menu item by the ideal recipe cost.

- **Standard food cost (SFC).** This is how you adjust for the unrealistically low PFC. The percentage includes unavoidable waste, employee meals, etc. This food-cost percentage is compared to the AFC and is the standard that management must meet.

- **Prime food cost includes the food cost with the cost of direct labor.** This is labor incurred because the item is made from scratch - baking pies and bread, trimming steaks, etc. When the food cost is determined for these items, the cost of the labor needed to prepare them is added. So prime cost is food cost plus necessary direct labor. This costing method is applied to every menu item needing extensive direct labor before it is served to the customer. Indirect labor cannot be attributed to any particular menu item and is, therefore, overhead. Prime cost is the total cost of food and beverage sold, payroll and employee benefits costs.

- **Beverage cost ratio is calculated when alcoholic beverages are sold.** It is determined by dividing costs by sales - calculated the same way as food consumed. A single beverage ratio can't be standardized because the percentage will vary depending on the mix of hard alcohol, wine and beer. Spirits run a lower cost percentage than wine and beer, and as such, it is recommended that alcoholic beverages be split into their three categories.

- **Beverage exclusions.** Beverage sales do not include coffee, tea, milk or juice, which are usually considered food. Wherever you include soft drinks, know that it will reduce the food cost, since the ratio of cost to selling price is so low.

Essential Sales and Turnover Calculations

In order to keep tight control of the financial side of your operation, you'll need to understand (and use) the following calculations:

- **Check average.** This calculation is not just total food and beverage sales divided by customers served. Of course, this is one way to determine your check average, but it is important to see how this figure compares to the check average you need to meet your daily sales goals. If you are coming in under what you need, you should look at your prices. Check average should be determined by each meal period, especially when different menus are served for each meal. Standards need to be set on how customers who order only a drink and no food are counted.

- **Seat turnover.** This refers to how many times you can fill a chair during a meal period with another customer. Restaurants with low check averages need high seat turnover.

- **Inventory turnover.** Inventory turnover is calculated by dividing cost of food consumed by your average inventory. (This is simply your beginning inventory plus your ending inventory, divided by two.)

- **Ratio of food-to-beverage sales.** This is simply the ratio of their percentages of your total sales. In restaurants with a higher percentage of beverages than food sales, profits are generally higher, because there is a greater profit margin on beverages.

- **Sales mix is the number of each menu item sold.** This is crucial to cost analysis because each item impacts food cost differently. If your Wendy's does a huge breakfast business and the one down the street does a big lunch, your food costs are going to be different than theirs.

- **Breakeven point (BEP) is simply when sales equal expenses.** Businesses can operate forever at break-even if there are no investors looking for a return on their money. To determine a breakeven analysis you need to break the costs into two categories: Fixed Costs and Variable Costs. Fixed costs remain constant regardless of sales volume and include items such as rent, insurance, property taxes and management payroll, etc.

Variable costs will increase or decrease in relation to sales changes and includes such items as food and beverage costs.

- **Contribution margin is your gross profit.** It is what remains after all expenses have been subtracted from 100-percent net.

- **Closing point.** Closing point is when the cost of being open for a given time period is more expensive than revenue earned. This means that if it cost you $2,000 to open today and you only made $1,800, your closing point expense will be $200.

- **Sales per square foot.** This refers to the total annual sales for the establishment divided by the total square footage for a given period. For example, the sales for the year are $1,000,000 the total square footage is 7,500; thus the sales per square foot is $133.33.

- **Income statement** (often called profit and loss statement or P & L). This is the scorecard for business. Part of a company's financial statements, it summarizes revenues and expenses during a specific period of time. It shows the revenue, expenses and profit or loss. It shows these things for some period of time, usually a month or a year. An income statement is usually titled: "Income Statement for X Business for the period ending December 31, 2003."

Profitability Ratios

Profitability is often measured in percentage terms in order to facilitate making comparisons of a company's financial performance against past year's performance and against the performance of other companies. When profitability is expressed as a percentage (or ratio), the new figures are called profit margins. The most common profit margins are all expressed as percentages of Net Sales. Let's look at a few of the most commonly used profit margins that you can easily learn to use to help you measure and compare firms:

- **Gross Margin** is the resulting percentage when Gross Profit is divided by Net Sales. Remember that Gross Profit is equal to Net Sales - Cost of Goods Sold. (Gross Profit ÷ Net Sales = Gross Margin). Therefore, Gross Margin represents the percentage of revenue remaining after Cost of Goods Sold is deducted. Let us take a look at a simple example. Net Sales = $1,000, Cost of Goods Sold = $400, Gross Profit = $600. In this example the Gross Margin = 600 ÷ 1000 = 0.60 or 60%. Since this ratio only takes into account sales and variable costs (Costs of Goods sold), this ratio is a good indicator of a restaurant's efficiency in producing and distributing its products. The higher the ratio, the higher the efficiency of the production process.

- **Operating Margin.** As the name implies, Operating Margin is the resulting ratio when Operating Income is divided by Net Sales. (Operating Income ÷ Net Sales = Operating Margin). This ratio measures the quality of a restaurant's operations. A restaurant with a high operating margin in relation to the industry average has operations that are more efficient. Typically, to achieve this result, the company must have lower fixed costs, a better Gross Margin, or a combination of the two. At any rate, companies that are more efficient than their competitors in their core operations have a distinct advantage. Efficiency is good. Advantages are even better.

- **Net Margin.** As the name implies, Net Margin is a measure of profitability for the sum of a restaurant's operations. It is equal to Net Profit divided by Net Sales: Net Profit ÷ Net Sales = Net Margin. As with the other ratios, you will want to compare Net Margin with other restaurants in the area and in the industry overall. This is where the National Restaurant Association's published report entitled The Operations Report, based on an annual survey of operator income statements conducted jointly by the Association and the accounting firm of Deloitte & Touche, provides detailed data on where the restaurant dollar comes from and where it goes. This is one reason that using the standard chart of accounts is so highly recommended. You can also track year-to-year changes in Net Margin to see if a company's competitive position is improving or getting worse.

- **The higher the net margin relative to the industry (or relative to past years), the better.** Often a high net margin indicates that the company you are examining is an efficient producer. However, as with all the previous profit margin measurements, you always need to check past years of performance. Strong profit margins that are sustainable indication that a company has been able to outperform their competitors consistently.

The Balance Sheet

Often referred to as the basic business financial statement, the balance sheet shows three things about a business: assets, liabilities and owner's equity. It is important to know the rules used in recording assets and liabilities and in constructing a balance sheet. It is also important to understand the proper and improper uses of this statement. If you don't know these things, either learn them or hire someone (a CPA) who can advise you. You'll need to understand the basic terminology:

- **Assets.** Assets are things that are owned by the business.

- **Liabilities.** Liabilities are things that are owed to others.

- **Owner's equity.** Owner's equity is the difference between assets and liabilities. Owner's equity can be thought of in this way: If the business were to liquidate all the assets and pay off all the liabilities, what is left would be owner's equity. The owner would have a right to keep this equity. The listing of assets on the balance sheet is customarily done at cost or adjusted cost. Inventory, a common asset, would be recorded at cost value even though it may be sold for more or less than cost in a liquidation situation. A building, another common asset, might have appreciated in value, but this added value would not be recognized on the balance sheet.

Why Should the Balance Sheet to Important to You?

Many restaurant operators often fail to look at the balance sheet. But, the balance sheet is the fundamental report of a company's possessions, debts and capital invested. The balance sheet is the first financial document your banker or investor will look at. You need to know that:

- **You can use the balance sheet to examine the following:**
    - Can the firm meet its financial obligations?
    - How much money has already been invested in this company?
    - Is the company overly indebted?
    - What kind of assets has the company purchased with its financing?

- **Liquidity Ratios.** The following liquidity ratios are all designed to measure a company's ability to cover its short-term obligations. Companies will generally pay their interest payments and other short-term debts with current assets. Therefore, it is essential that a firm have an adequate surplus of current assets in order to meet their current liabilities. If a company has only liquid assets, it may not be able to make payments on their debts. To measure a firm's ability to meet such short-term obligations, various ratios have been developed.

- **You will need to study the following balance sheet ratios:**
    - Current ratio
    - Acid test (or quick ratio)
    - Working capital
    - Leverage

- **Current Ratio.** The Current Ratio measures a firm's ability to pay their current obligations. The greater extent to which current assets exceed current liabilities, the easier a company can meet its short-term obligations. (Current Assets ÷ Current Liabilities = Current Ratio.) After calculating the Current Ratio, you should compare it with other restaurants. A ratio lower than that of the industry average suggests that the company may have liquidity problems. However, a significantly higher ratio may suggest that the company is not efficiently using its funds. A satisfactory Current Ratio for a company will be within close range of the industry average, which for most restaurants is between 0.5 and 1.25. This is much lower than most other industries, but keep in mind that the restaurant business is mostly a cash business and can operate quite well with a lower ratio.

- **Acid Test or Quick Ratio.** The Acid Test Ratio or Quick Ratio is very similar to the Current Ratio except for the fact that it excludes inventory. For this reason, it's also a more conservative ratio. (Current Assets - Inventory ÷ Current Liabilities = Acid Test.) Inventory is excluded in this ratio, because inventory cannot always be quickly converted to cash.

- **Working Capital.** Working Capital is simply the amount that Current Assets exceed Current Liabilities. Here it is in the form of the equation: (Current Assets - Current Liabilities = Working Capital.) The working capital formula is very similar to the current ratio. The only difference is that it gives you a dollar amount rather than a ratio. It, too, is calculated to determine a firm's ability to pay its short-term obligations. Working

Capital can be viewed as somewhat of a security blanket. The greater the amount of Working Capital, the more security an investor has and assurance that they'll be able to meet their financial obligations.

- **Debt.** Many times a company does not have enough liquidity. This is often the cause of being over leveraged (debt).

The Statement of Cash Flows

The simplest form of a statement of cash flows is a listing of cash coming into the business and cash going out. Think of a checkbook register. You record cash that you deposit into your bank account and you record each check that you write. You don't record anything else – just cash you get and cash you pay out. You need to know the following facts about cash flow statements:

- **The rules.** With business cash flow, the same simple rule applies. If it is either cash received or cash paid, it is listed. If it is not cash, it is not listed. Selling something on account and not getting the money is not a statement of cash flows transaction. If something is purchased, but no cash is paid, it is not recorded on the statement of cash flows until the cash is actually paid out. Of course, one of the great aspects of the restaurant business is that it is primarily, if not exclusively, a cash business.

- **A statement of cash flows is different from an income statement** (profit and loss statement). The latter is kept on the accrual basis of accounting.

Accrual accounting, which is used with most businesses and all businesses with inventory, recognizes sales when they are made, even if the cash is collected at a later time. It also recognizes expenses when incurred even if paid 30 or 60 days later.

- **Other expenditure.** There is spending in business that is not immediately reflected on the income statement. When inventory is purchased, there is no entry on the income statement even if cash is paid for the purchase. When equipment is bought with cash, only a part of that purchase is usually reflected in the current income statement. The rest is shown on future statements by way of depreciation expense. These types of transactions would show up on a statement of cash flows, but NOT on an income statement.

- **Four-week accounting period.** Companies typically close their books and prepare financial statements at the end of each month. The problem for a retail business, such as a restaurant, is that there are uneven number of days and uneven number of the type of days in a month. For example, you may have an extra Saturday, which would skew numbers upwards. Consider using a four-week accounting period so you can compare apples to apples.

- **EBITDA.** This refers to earnings before interest, tax, depreciation and amortization (profit before any interest, taxes, depreciation or amortization) have been deducted.

Simple Tactics to Help You Compile Your Financial Reports - Faster!

- **Get a computer** – the best you can afford.

- **Get a great software package** such as QuickBooks and a POS system.

- **Order Tasty Profits** or use the National Restaurant Association's chart of accounts in conjunction with your accounting software.

- **Close the accounting period internally,** using a four-week accounting period, don't wait for your accountant. Use your CPA to assist in quarterly reports, end-of-year and tax planning.

- **Utilize online banking services** – including bank account reconciliation.

- **Have missing documents faxed or e-mailed to you** – if necessary, estimate, you can adjust later.

- **Do you bookkeeping daily** yourself, so it doesn't get away from you.

- **POS systems should be linked to your accounting software.**

- **Time clocks should be linked to your accounting software** and possibly to your POS system.

Controlling Food Costs

In order to control food costs effectively, there are four essential things that you need to do. First, forecast how much and what you are going to sell. Second, purchase and prepare according to these forecasts. Third, portion effectively. Finally, control waste and theft. Consider the following:

- **Standards.** In order to do these effectively, you must have standards to which you rigorously adhere. Here are several standards that will help you sustain quality, consistency and low cost:

- **Don't allow chefs to determine pricing.** The plates your chefs create are their pride and joy. But don't let them set prices.

- **Standardized recipes.** Since the recipe is the basis for determining the cost of a menu item, standard recipes will assure consistent quality and cost. Standardized recipes include ingredients, preparation methods, yield, equipment used and plate presentation.

- **Standardized purchase specifications.** These are detailed descriptions of the ingredients used in your standardized recipes. Quality and price of all ingredients are known and agreed upon before purchases are made, making the recipe's cost consistent from unit to unit and week to week.

Yield Costs

Once you have standardized recipes in place, you can determine the per-plate cost of every dish. In order to do this, you need to know the basic ingredients' cost and the edible yield of those ingredients for each dish. There are a number of necessary terms for this process:

- **As-Purchased (AP) Weight.** The weight of the product as delivered, including bones, trim, etc.

- **Edible-Portion (EP) Weight.** The amount of weight or volume that is available to be portioned after carving or cooking.

- **Waste.** The amount of usable product that is lost due to processing, cooking or portioning, as well as usable by-products that have no salable value.

- **Usable Trim.** Processing by-products that can be sold as other menu items. These recover a portion of or all of their cost.

- **Yield.** The net weight or volume of food after processing but before portioning.

- **Standard Yield.** The yield generated by standardized recipes and portioning procedures – how much usable product remains after processing and cooking.

- **Standard Portion.** The size of the portion according to the standardized recipe, also the basis for determining the cost of the plated portion.

- **Convenience Foods.** Items where at least a portion of the preparation labor is done before delivery. These can include pre-cut chicken, ready-made dough, etc.

- **These factors allow you to calculate plate costs.** The cost of convenience foods are higher than if you made them from scratch, but once you factor in labor, necessary equipment, inventories of ingredients, more complicated purchasing and storage, etc., you may find that these foods offer considerable savings.

- **Costing convenience foods.** To cost convenience foods, you simply count, weigh or measure the portion size and determine how many portions there are. Then divide the number of servable portions into the as-purchased price. Even with their pre-preparation, a small allowance for normal waste must be factored in, often as little as 2 percent per yield.

- **Costing items from scratch** is a little more complex. Most menu items require processing that causes shrinkage of some kind. As a result, if the weight or volume of the cooked product is less than the as-purchased (AP) weight, the edible portion (EP) cost will be higher than the AP price. It's a simple addition of the labor involved and the amount of salable product being reduced. Through this process, your buyer uses yields to determine quantities to purchase and your chef discovers optimum quantities to order that result in the highest yield and the least waste.

*Your menu should
positively affect the
revenue and
operational efficiency
of your restaurant.*

CHAPTER THREE

A FINANCIALLY PROFITABLE MENU

Menu Sales Mix

The menu is where you begin to design a restaurant. If you have a specific menu idea, your restaurant's location must be carefully planned to ensure customer traffic will support your concept. This also works the other way: If you already have the location, design your menu around the customers you want to attract. Consider the following basic requirements:

- **Functionality.** Once your concept is decided, your equipment and kitchen space requirements should be designed around the recipes on your menu. Once a kitchen has been built, there is, of course, some flexibility to menu changes, but new pieces of equipment may be impossible to add without high costs or renovations. To design correctly, you need to visualize delivery, processing, preparation, presentation and washing. To do this, you must be intimately familiar with each menu item.

- **Fit for purpose.** When shopping for equipment, choose based on the best equipment for your needs, not price. Only when you have decided if you need a small non-vented fryer or an industrial one, two ovens or five, and then which specific brand will meet your needs, should you begin to find the best price. This is true for equipment all the way down to pots, pans, dishes and utensils.

The Menu Itself

Your menu should not just be a list of the dishes you sell, it should positively affect the revenue and operational efficiency of your restaurant. Start by selecting dishes that reflect your customer's preferences and emphasize what your staff does well. Attempting to cater to everyone generally has you doing nothing particularly well and doesn't distinguish your restaurant. Your menu should be a major communicator of the concept and personality of your restaurant, as well as an important cost control. Bear in mind the following:

- **Design.** A well-designed menu creates an accurate image of the restaurant in a customer's head, even before the customer has been inside. It also directs the attention to certain selections and increases the chances of them being ordered. Your menu also determines, depending upon its complexity and sophistication, how detailed your cost-control system needs to be.

- **An effective menu does five key things:**
  1. Emphasizes what customers want and what you do best.
  2. Is an effective communication, merchandising and cost-control tool.
  3. Obtains the necessary check average for sales and profits.
  4. Uses staff and equipment efficiently.
  5. Makes forecasting sales more consistent and accurate for purchasing, preparation and scheduling.

- **Plan to have a menu that works for you.** The design of your menu will directly affect whether it achieves these goals. Don't leave this to chance.

Certain practices can influence the choices your guests make. Instead of randomly placing items on the menu, single out and emphasize the items you want to sell. These will generally be dishes with low food cost and high profits that are easy to prepare. Once you have chosen these dishes, use design – print style, paper color and graphic design – to direct the readers' attention to these items. In general, a customer's eye will fall to the middle of the page first. This is an important factor. However, design elements used to draw a reader's eye to another part of the menu can be effective as well. Also, customers remember the first and last things they read more than anything else, so drawing their eyes to specific items is also important.

- **Print the menu in-house.** With today's desktop publishing technology, you can easily produce your own menus. All you need is a software program like Menu Pro, available at www.atlantic-pub.com. Choose from a selection of menu papers at www.ideaart.com or www.armesco.com.

- **Tell your story on the back of the menu.** People always want to know more. Use this chance to increase their value and perception of your restaurant quality. Tell them how your staff prepares fresh salad ingredients on a daily basis, never using pre-made items or canned goods. Let them know that you grind fresh gourmet coffee beans each morning before coffee is brewed. Tell your story and your guests will be impressed.

- **Provide clean, presentable menus.** Ensure that your menus are always clean and appear to be as good as new, otherwise, throw them out. Greasy, sticky, soiled menus with bad creases, dog-ears and glass ring stains are not very appealing to people who are preparing to dine. If a server hands a sticky, dirty menu to a customer, what kind of impression do you think that customer will have of your restaurant?

Menu "Do Nots"

- **Don't charge extra for the small items.** Some restaurants will charge an additional $0.30 for a slice of cheese on their hamburger or $0.40 for blue cheese dressing. While it may cost you a bit extra for these items, you should cover the cost by averaging it in on the overall cost of the meal. When you break down charges like this, people get the impression that you are being petty.

- **Don't tell your guests that you've run out of a particular item.** You've sold out, not run out. That makes it sound as if the restaurant is poorly managed and unprepared. Instead, make sure you tell them that you've sold out of that item because it has been so popular. Selling out is a good thing, not a bad thing. It means business is good and food is fresh.

Analyze and Classify Your Menu Sales Mix

Once you have an effective menu design, analyzing your sales mix to determine the impact each item has on sales, costs and profits is an important practice. If you have costs and waste under control, looking at your menu sales mix can help you further reduce costs and boost profits. You will find that some items need to be promoted more aggressively, while others need to be dropped altogether. Classifying your menu items is necessary for making those decisions. Here are some suggested classifications:

- **Primes.** These are popular items that are low in food cost and high in profit. Have them stand out on your menu.

- **Standards.** Items with high food costs and high profit margins. You can possibly raise the price on this item and push it as a signature.

- **Sleepers.** Slow-selling low food-cost items with low profit margins. Work to increase the likelihood that these will be seen and ordered through more prominent menu display, featured on menu boards, lowered prices, etc.

- **Problems.** High in food cost and low in profits. If you can, raise the price and lower production cost. If you can't, hide them on the menu. If sales don't pick up, get rid of them altogether.

Prices that are too high will drive customers away.

CHAPTER FOUR

PRICING SUCCESSFULLY

Pricing

Pricing is an important aspect of your revenues and customer counts. Prices that are too high will drive customers away and prices that are too low will kill your profits. But pricing is not the simple matter of an appropriate markup over cost; it combines other factors as well. Price can either be market driven or demand driven:

- **Market-driven prices must be responsive** to your competitors' prices. Common dishes that both you and the place down the road sell need to be priced competitively. This is also true when you're introducing new items for which a demand has not been developed.

- **Opposite to these are demand-driven items.** These are items which customers ask for and where demand exceeds your supply. You have a short-term monopoly on these items and, therefore, price is driven up until demand slows or competitors begin to sell similar items.

- **Markup.** A combination of methods is usually a good idea, since each menu item is usually different. Two basic theories are: charge as much as you can, and charge as little as you can. Each has its pluses and minuses. Obviously, if you charge as much as you can, you increase the chance of greater profits. You do, however, run the risk of needing to offer a product those customers feel is worth the price; otherwise you will lose them because they won't think you're a good value. Charging the lowest price you can gives customers a great sense of value but lowers your profit margin per item.

Determining Prices

Prices are generally determined by competition and demand. Your prices must be in line with the category in which customers place you. Fast-food burrito joints don't price like a five-star restaurant and vice versa. Both would lose their customer base if they did. While this is an exaggeration, the point is still the same: You want your customers to know that your image and your prices fit into that picture. Here are four ways to determine prices:

- **Competitive pricing.** Simply based on meeting or beating your competition's prices. This is an ineffective method, since it assumes diners are making their choice on price alone and not food quality, ambiance, service, etc.

- **Intuitive pricing.** This means you don't want to take the time to find out what your competition is charging, so you are charging based on what you feel guests are willing to pay. If your sense of the value of your product is good, then it works. Otherwise, it can be problematic.

- **Psychological pricing.** Price is more of a factor to lower-income customers who go to lower-priced restaurants. If they don't know an item is good, they assume it is if it's expensive. If you change your prices, the order in which buyers see them also affects their perceptions. If an item was initially more expensive, it will be viewed as a bargain and vice versa.

- **Trial-and-error pricing.** This is based on customer reactions to prices. It is not practical in terms of determining your overall prices, but can be effective with individual items to bring them closer to the price a customer is willing to pay, or to distinguish them from similar menu items with a higher or lower food cost.

Other Factors That Will Help You Determine Prices

Whether customers view you as a leader or a follower can make a big difference regarding how they view your prices. If people think of you as the best seafood restaurant in the area, they'll be willing to pay a little more. Here are some other considerations:

- **Service determines people's sense of value.** This is even truer when the difference in actual food quality between you and the competition is negligible. If your customers order at a counter and bus their own tables, this lack of service cost needs to be reflected in your prices. Also, in a competitive market, providing great service can be a factor that puts you in a leadership position and allows you to charge a higher price.

- **Other considerations.** Location, ambiance, customer base, product presentation and desired check average all factor into what you feel you can charge and what you need to charge to make a profit.

Internal Controls

It is estimated that about five cents on every dollar spent in U.S. restaurants is lost to theft. Clearly established and followed controls can lessen this percentage. Begin by separating duties and recording every transaction. If these basic systems are in place, then workers know at each step of the way that they will be held responsible for shrinkage. Management Information Systems (MIS) are common tools for accumulating, analyzing and reporting data. They help establish proper rules for consistent and prompt reporting and set up efficient flows of paperwork and data collection. In short, their goal is to prevent fraud on all levels. While no system is perfect, a good MIS will show where fraud or loss is occurring, allowing you to remedy the situation. Consider the following issues:

- **In most restaurants, the majority of internal theft occurs in and around the bar.** In tightly run establishments, cash is more likely to be taken by management than hourly workers, because managers have access to it and know the system well. Hourly workers tend to steal items, not cash, because that's what they can get their hands on. Keeping food away from the back door and notifying your employees when you are aware of theft and are investigating can have a deterring effect.

- **The key to statistical control is entering transactions into the system.** This can be done electronically or by hand. Either way, if food or beverages can be consumed without being entered into the system, your system is flawed and control is compromised.

- **Five other cost-control concepts are crucial to your control system:**
  - Documentation of tasks, activities and transactions must be required.

  - Supervision and review of employees by management intimately familiar with set performance standards.

  - Splitting of duties so no single person is involved in all parts of the task cycle.

  - Timeliness. All tasks must be done within set time guidelines; comparisons then made at established control points. Reports must be made at scheduled times to detect problems.

  - Cost-benefit relationships. Cost of procedures used to benefits gained must exceed the cost of implementing the controls.

- **Control procedures.** The basic control procedure is an independent verification at a control point during and after the completion of a task. This is often done through written or electronic reports. Verification determines if the person performing the task has authority to do so and if the quantity and quality available and performance results meet set standards.

- **Point-of-sale systems are crucial for reducing loss.** If your servers simply can't obtain any food or beverage without a hard-copy check, or without entering the sale electronically, you have eliminated most of their opportunity to steal. Many electronic systems are available in the industry and, once initial training and intimidation are overcome, they can seriously reduce the amount of theft and shrinkage in your restaurant. These systems also allow you to see, instantly, which items are selling best at different times of the day. This enables you to order more efficiently, keep inventory to a minimum and automatically subtract from inventory all the ingredients used in the items you sold. These can be invaluable tools for tracking employee productivity, initiating promotions and contests and generating weekly, daily, by meal or hourly sales reports. Point-of-sale systems collect invaluable data for you to interpret.

Purchasing and Ordering

What exactly is the difference? Purchasing is setting the policy on which suppliers, brands, grades and varieties of products will be ordered. These are your standardized purchase specifications; the specifics of how items are delivered, paid for, returned, etc., negotiated between management and distributors. Basically, purchasing is what you order and from whom. Ordering, then, is simply the act of contacting the suppliers and notifying them of the quantity you require. This is a simpler, lower-level task. Here are the basics:

- **Develop a purchasing program.** Once menus have been created that meet your customers' satisfaction and your profit needs, develop a purchasing program that assures your profit margins.

- **An efficient purchasing program incorporates:** Standard purchase specifications based on standardized recipes. Standardized yields and portion control that allow for accurate costs based on portions actually served.

- **Ordering.** To order the necessary supplies, your

operator needs to be able to predict how much will be needed to maintain purchase specifications, follow standard recipes and enforce portioning standards. When these are done well, optimum quantities can be kept on hand.

- **Buying also has its own distinctions.** Open or informal buying is face-to-face or over-the-phone contact and uses largely oral negotiations and purchase specifics. In formal buying, terms are put in writing and payment invoices are stated as conditions for price quotes and customer-service commitments. Its customer service is possibly the most important aspect of the supplier you choose, because good sales representatives know their products, have an understanding of your needs and offer helpful suggestions.

Inventory, Storage and Accounts Payable

Ordering effectively is impossible unless you know your inventory. Before an order is placed, counts of stock should be made. Many software programs are able to determine order quantities directly from sales reports, but without this kind of system, you must inventory what you have on hand before ordering. The taking of inventory must be streamlined, because it must be done as frequently as you order. It mustn't be an unpleasant late-night debacle that is done only rarely and only when it has to be. Whether your inventory system is by hand or computer, its purpose is to accomplish the following:

- Provide records of what you need.
- Provide records of product specifications.
- Provide records of suppliers.
- Provide records of prices and unit of purchase.
- Provide a record of product use levels.

57

- Facilitate efficient ordering.
- Increase the accuracy of inventory.
- Facilitate the inventory process.
- Make it easy to detect variance levels in inventory.

- **Records and reports.** With such a system, the records generated and kept are extensive and valuable. You will have records of what you purchased, product specifications, your primary and alternative suppliers, price and unit of purchase. Equally important, reports will indicate the par usage level between deliveries. These statistics allow for month-to-month comparisons to be made between units in a multi-unit operation.

Labor Productivity

Labor costs and turnover are serious concerns in today's restaurant market. Increasing labor costs cannot be offset by continuously higher prices. Maximizing worker productivity, so few can do more, has become a key challenge to the restaurateur. This is especially true since the food service industry continues to be an entry-level arena for the unskilled and often uneducated. Qualified applicants are still few in the restaurant industry. A few of the causes of high labor costs and low productivity are poor layout and design of your operation, lack of labor-saving equipment, poor scheduling and no regular detailed system to collect and analyze payroll data. The following are some suggested ways management could improve these areas for greater efficiency:

- **Scheduling.** The key to controlling labor costs is not a low average-hourly wage, but proper scheduling of productive employees. Place your best servers, cooks, etc., where you need them most. This requires knowing the strengths and weaknesses of your employees. Staggering the arrival and departure of employees is a good way to follow the volume of expected customers and to minimize labor costs during slow times. Use scheduling software such as Employee Schedule Partner, www.atlantic-pub.com. Some POS systems have scheduling software built into them.

- **On-call scheduling.** When your forecasted customer counts are inaccurate, scheduled labor must be adjusted up or down to meet productivity standards. Employees simply wait at home to be called if they are needed for work. If they don't receive a call by a certain time, they know they're not needed. Employees prefer this greatly to coming in only to be sent home and by tipped staff that don't want to work when business is slow.

- **On-break schedules.** When you can't send employees home, put them on a 30-minute break. Include a meal. Deduct the 30 minutes from their timecards and take a credit for the cost of the meal against the minimum wage.

Pricing Beverages

Pricing beverages is not just a cost-markup exercise. The markup of alcohol in restaurants is often lower than in bars where liquor makes up the majority of sales. Prices reflect the uniqueness of an operation and the overhead operating costs. Monitor your liquor costs accurately:

- **Record the sales of each type of beverage**

separately. Use separate keys for wine, beer and spirits on your register or point-of-sale system. Unless an electronic system is used, however, a detailed sales mix is difficult to obtain.

• **Responsibility.** Make your alcoholic beverage purchaser or buyer responsible for ensuring that adequate amounts of required spirits are on hand.

• **Unlike food and supplies, purchasers are not required to shop around for the best deal** for the following reasons:
   • Specific dealers only sell specific brands.

   • Wholesaling of alcohol is state regulated and controlled.

   • Prices are published in monthly journals, and there is little change from month to month.

   • Only quantity discounts are available.

   • Purchase is done by brand name.

Beverage Inventory Control

Although purchasing and ordering alcohol is much simpler than purchasing and ordering food, the need to inventory correctly is no less crucial. In fact, alcohol needs to be guarded and inventoried more rigorously because of its cost, ease of theft and possible abuses. Liquor inventory should be kept locked in different storerooms, cages or walk-ins than other inventory. Only authorized individuals should have access to these areas and requisitions must be filled out to record withdrawals. Other tips include:

- **Replenish your stock from "stamped" or marked empty bottles.** These prevent bartenders from bringing their own bottles in and selling them. If this does occur, it's virtually impossible to detect without marked bottles, because there will be no inventory shortages. If you have drops in sales levels of $50-$100 in one night, these are signs of phantom bottles in your inventory.

- **Auditing.** Inventories need to be audited to ensure your liquor is actually in the storeroom, and deliveries need to be checked for accuracy. It is recommended that a purchase order, not the driver's invoice, be used to verify deliveries. Controls for determining dispensing costs, recording sales and accounting for consumed beverages can be done three different ways:

- **Automated systems that dispense and count.** Systems range from mechanical dispensers attached to each bottle, to magnetic pourers that can only be activated by the register. These systems are exact, reduce spillage and cannot give free drinks. Basically, liquor can't be dispensed without being put into the system.

- **Ounce or drink controls.** This requires establishing standard glassware and recipes, recording each drink sold, determining costs of each drink, comparing actual use levels to potential consumption levels and comparing actual drink cost percent to potential cost percent.

- **Par stock or bottle control.** This is a matter of keeping the maximum amount of each type of liquor behind the bar, then turning in all empty bottles for full ones. No full bottles are given without an empty one coming in. A standard sales value per bottle is determined based on the drinks it makes. A sales value is determined from consumption and compared to actual sales for variances. If less was sold than consumed, investigate.

- **Standards at the bar are as important as in the kitchen.** Dispensers, jiggers or other measuring devices should be mandated to assure portion controls. Regular inventory also needs to be done to watch for fraud and theft. Management needs to be expected to meet set standards. Whenever a manager changes shift, you must verify inventory to make sure that numbers reported are "actual" and haven't been adjusted to meet costs.

CHAPTER FIVE

PLEASING CUSTOMERS

Service Guarantees

You've got to guarantee specific services to build up trust and loyalty among your customers. Service guarantees require you to:

- Focus on results
- Set standards
- Generate feedback
- Acknowledge failures

- **Use your guarantee as a yardstick.** By setting a standard, you have quantifiable standards by which to measure your service. For example, if you guarantee customers their order within 15 minutes of placing it, then you now have a result to achieve and a standard to live up to. One minute over those first 15 minutes forces you to acknowledge failure.

- **Learn from your failures.** A service guarantee gives you something that can actually be measured and results that are easy to see. It also helps refine and improve upon your existing service and procedures.

Meeting Expectations - First Impressions

Identify customer needs and expectations. Set yourself apart – from day one. Here are some simple tips:

- **Identify demand.** Recognize that your guests have expectations of your service and make preparations based on three main criteria:
  - Price
  - Quality of food and presentation
  - Location

- **Identify expectations.** Make sure that price reflects service. If your check average is $6.25, they probably expect fast food, paper napkins or even plastic utensils - they may even expect to pour their own ice and drinks. At that price, self-service is quite acceptable. However, if customers spend $25, expectations are rather different. Diners paying higher prices don't expect to pour their own drinks. In fact, they'd expect to have their glasses refilled by the time they were half empty!

- **Exceed expectations.** Include a complimentary appetizer, a free glass of wine, free valet parking or umbrellas when it rains.

- **Insist on exceptional behavior and manners from your waitstaff.** This applies particularly to the front-of-the-house. Courtesy costs nothing.

- **Timely arrival of food.** Make sure that all food is served promptly at the correct temperature.

- **Ambiance.** Offer an ambiance that meets guest expectations. A pleasant welcome, comfort and cleanliness are the main factors by which your establishment is judged. But, of course, small, individual touches can set your restaurant apart.

- **Directions.** When people call for directions to your

restaurant, ask them if they have a fax machine or e-mail. It's much easier to send written instructions. Have some pre-printed direction sheets, or a standard e-mail text ready. If, however, you have to explain over the phone, be sure to give them land marks to look for in addition to street names. Have the directions on your Web site. Link to Web sites that provide directions for your customers.

Customer Response – Actively Seek Feedback

Feedback is very important. Take the initiative to talk to your guests:

- **Feedback surveys.** These have their place, but a lot of people don't bother to fill them out, as they've developed the impression that they aren't taken seriously. Be seen to respond. Go and speak with your customers – you will learn.

- **Manager presence.** Guests always enjoy talking to the manager or owner. If they aren't happy about something, they will not always tell the waitstaff and if they are told, the waitstaff may not tell you. Walk around and ask them if they are enjoying their meal and the service they're receiving.

- **Attentive waitstaff.** Don't tolerate the quick throw-away line, "Everything OK?" as staff whisk past the table, with no intention of waiting for a response. Be different – train staff to stop, listen and respond.

- **Hire a well-known chef to design your menu.** Hiring a well-known chef to design your menu will gain attention from the media, the restaurant industry and especially local customers within the area. Use the example from the golf courses – designed by Arnold Palmer or Jack Nicklaus. In other words, the chef can design the menu, but not actually be there to cook it.

- **Send a thank-you note.** For customers who fill out surveys, guest cards and other personal information, send them a simple thank-you note for their efforts. If you have their personal contact information, you could also send out thank-you notes to people just because they chose to dine at your restaurant.

Better Service, More Tips - Fifteen Top Tips!

Go beyond service expectations and your staff will see more tips. You will see more revenue. Good service is the difference between receiving 10 percent and 30 percent. Here are 15 top tips for increasing your gratuities:

- **Be competent and confident.** Get to grips with the menu. Prove that you're capable of describing every single dish in a way that makes your customers crave the food from your description. Also, show that you can juggle multiple tasks and requests, without faltering or slowing down.

- **Greet customers immediately.** No matter how busy you might be, take a moment to greet your guests within the first 2 minutes of them being seated. This lets them know you are aware of their existence and that they have been acknowledged. Let them know that you will be right with them in a few moments. Don't ignore them just because you can't take their order at that precise minute. You can still greet them and put them at ease.

- **Direct eye contact.** Whenever you're addressing multiple guests at a table, look into the eyes of the individual to whom you are speaking. If you are addressing the entire table, be sure to shift your gaze to everyone present so that they all feel they are being included in the discussion. Don't talk or greet them as you are moving away or walking by. Stop and give them your undivided attention, even if only for a few seconds.

- **Remember names and use them.** If a guest gives you their name, use it. Whenever it feels appropriate, address a customer by their name, especially if they're a regular. If a customer leaves a personal information card, or even if they happen to be wearing a business name tag during their lunch break, show them that you've noticed. It makes them feel more comfortable with you as their server.

- **Remember preferences.** When a customer returns, greet them as if you know them well and try to recall their likes and dislikes. Remember, for instance, how they prefer their food prepared.

- **Give a recommendation.** Offer a recommendation on the menu that you like the best. Encourage them to tell you what kinds of foods they like. Make another recommendation based on what they've just told you.

- **Introduce yourself creatively.** First, introduce the food and the specials. Start by telling them about your favorites on the menu. Once you've engaged their attention and sparked their interest, then introduce yourself. When you first approach a table and start with the standard, "Good evening, my name is Jack and I'll be your waiter tonight," they aren't paying attention to who you are and they don't really care. Five minutes later most of them probably still won't know your name.

- **Offer special comforts to single diners.** Offer them the newspaper. If they already have reading material or paperwork, try seating them in a well-lit area. If they seem inclined to talk, linger a little longer than you normally would and chat with them.

- **Leave extra napkins.** Always leave three to four napkins per person at a table. One or two napkins are never enough. Finger foods require getting messy, children are bound to make lots of messes and some people simply don't like wiping their hands and fingers or mouth on the same napkin more than once.

- **Replace used silverware.** Whenever you clear the table of appetizers, a salad or soup before the main course, ensure that you also remove the dirty silverware. Bring clean silverware to the table, immediately. Don't expect your guests to use the same silverware for dessert or the main course.

- **Recognize left-handed patrons.** If you notice a customer re-setting their glass and silverware on the opposite side from where you have placed them, then follow their example for anything else you bring them. Most likely, they are left-handed and will appreciate your attentiveness.

- **Place coffee cups in a ready-to-grasp position.**

While this is only a small gesture, the extra effort will be noticed and rewarded at the end of the meal.

- **Ask permission before pouring refills.** This shows attentiveness without hassling the guests. Always use a fresh cup for coffee and tea refills.

- **Settle the check promptly.** When guests indicate that they are ready to go, try to settle the check as promptly as possible. Don't make them wait.

- **Provide calculators at check time.** Provide a credit card-size calculator inside the folder of the bill or attach it to the tray with the bill. People come to your restaurant to relax and for enjoyment. The last thing they want is to calculate math in their heads. Groups sometimes need to split costs of appetizers, desserts and drinks in addition to their meal.

Provide Taste Samples

Nothing beats the experience. Allow your guests to taste samples before they actually order. This can be done for actual meals, desserts and especially wine. The following suggestions should give you ideas on how to develop this system within your own restaurant:

- **Appoint an employee.** Choose one employee to handle the sampling for each shift. For improved guest interaction, try to pick a member of staff with an outgoing personality and an easy smile. Offer this person a bonus or percentage of each additional sale they make as a result of the samples they display and urge customers to try.

- **Use unique serving platters.** Use serving platters that are decorative and reflect the image of your restaurant or the sample items on display. Be bold! You want them to attract attention as your server goes from table to table. Be creative and use coordinated colors that blend well together.

- **Create small portions.** Cut all samples into tiny portions. Provide each guest with a small plate or napkin. The idea is to whet appetites and convince guests to try something new.

- **Provide "samplers" with unique uniform or a few different accessories.** Make them visually appealing. Complement the restaurant theme or ambiance. For example, if the sampler has a platter full of seafood, then a nifty sailor outfit would be perfect.

- **Practice the selling script.** Before samplers go out on the floor, have them practice their script, how they should approach customers and the best way to phrase answers to potential questions. Descriptions should be credible and sound natural, not rehearsed. Ensure that your samplers are in the business of show selling - that means that their presentation should be as good as the food itself.

Healthy Food Preparation and Cooking – Without Sacrificing Taste and Flavor!

The way food is prepared is very important to many people. Your restaurant and your staff must adapt to the demands of change. Consider the following:

- **Cooking methods mean healthier choices.** More people are becoming health conscious but, at the same time, don't want to give up the luxury of great taste! Instead of deep-frying, bake items such as French fries in the oven. Offer steamed vegetables. Use healthier cooking oils and ingredients.

- **Cut out the fat in beef.** Order lean cuts of beef such as top round, tenderloin or sirloin. Have your kitchen staff trim all visible fat before cooking. Use extra lean ground sirloin for casseroles, chili, tacos, spaghetti sauces and skillet dishes. If you have cooked ground beef, throw it in a strainer and rinse it well with hot water. Substitute ground beef with turkey. These simple tips can lower the fat intake by as much as 50 percent! But tell your customers what you are doing.

- **Use nonstick pans.** You need to invest in some nonstick pans. If necessary use cooking sprays, which are less fattening and healthier.

- **Drip the fat away.** Place a rack inside the pan when cooking or baking beef. This allows most of the fat to drip away from the meat.

- **Use stock or broth.** Try basting or searing beef with stock or broth instead of oil. Also, create great-tasting sauces for beef roasts by adding stock or broth into the pan juice. Bring it to a quick boil for thickness and then add your seasoning and herbs or a touch of wine.

- **Substitute oils**. Whenever a recipe calls for oil, substitute with a combination of flavored oils, herbs or stock. Fresh garlic, hot and sweet peppers

71

as well as fresh ginger are great for adding flavor without the fat. Create some great unique recipes by experimenting with a variety of combinations.

- **Use more marinades.** To add ethnic flavor, use more marinades, which also tenderize and enhance the flavor of food. You can cook healthily without involving a great deal of extra time and effort. Cater to guests' needs and wants.

- **Cook with low-fat cheese.** Try using low-fat or reduced-fat cheese in some recipes that call for cheese. To enhance flavor, sprinkle fresh-grated Romano or Parmesan cheese. Make sure your guests are not faced with sacrificing taste for a healthier meal.

- **Reducing fat content.** If you must use oil, use it sparingly. Put the oil in a spray bottle and spray just a little on a slice of bread before toasting. Instead of using shortening, use vegetable oil and reduce the amount called for in the recipe by at least a fourth. These are simple steps that you can take for your low-fat menus.

- **Lowering cholesterol.** If guests are ordering from a low-fat menu, they could also have high-cholesterol problems. Therefore, prepare the food with that in mind. For recipes with eggs, substitute two egg whites for each egg.

- **Lighter desserts.** Serve cake with pudding or fruit topping instead of frosting. Use fruits for moistness rather than glaze. When appropriate, use vanilla extract as a sweetener instead of sugar.

CHAPTER SIX

THE RESTAURANT INTERIOR

A Place to Impress

The way that your restaurant is designed and the layout of your dining room floor can make or break your business. Consider the following type of arrangements when opening a new restaurant or instigating renovations. You may be surprised at the difference a few alterations and additions can make:

- **Environment does make a difference.** Position the doorway entrance directly in front of the pedestrian sidewalk traffic. Most doorways are located horizontally, but if you redesign your entrance at an angle, it creates a more welcoming first impression.

- **Energy flowing arrangements.** Have a curve-based bar design. A bar with a straight design gives the impression of rigidity and inflexibility, while a curve-based design exhibits a feeling of harmony and symmetry. It projects a community atmosphere and builds more welcoming warmth.

- **Best Restaurant Equipment & Design,** www.bestrestaurant.com, 800-837-2378, has a history of designing such restaurants as Applebee's, Bennigan's, T.G.I. Friday's and Ponderosa Steakhouse.

- **Milton Architects,** www.miltonarchitects.com, 713-522-4171, specializes in commercial designs for restaurants and retail buildings.

- **Butler Lemons Design,** www.blr-arch.com, 407-648-8888, provides specialty architect design for themed restaurants.

- **Coe Construction, Inc,** www.coeconstruction.com, 970-663-7336, specializes in new construction and remodeling of restaurants.

Create a More Inviting Ambiance

Ever sat in an empty room where you could hear your conversation literally bouncing off the walls? An empty restaurant might persuade your guests that people aren't eating there for a reason. Try enhancing your bare dining area by creating an impression of a cozy, full dining room:

- **Use moveable room dividers.** Install moveable walls or room dividers. This gives you flexibility, with the option to remove the dividers when your restaurant is at full capacity. Create a "smaller" dining room at slower hours of business. Your guests will hardly notice the difference as long as the transition is quietly and smoothly executed.

- **Visual elements.** Introduce visual elements such as plants, trees, mirrors, curtains and other artistic objects. It helps to break up the room into smaller, interesting sections.

- **Background music.** Soft background music can

help to eliminate the echo effect of voices, laughter and other noises. Loud music can be just as distracting as the absence of noise. Try adjusting the volume so that it meshes with all the background noise without completely drowning out the conversation of those sitting at a table together.

- **Adjust lighting levels.** Ever noticed how many elegant restaurants have dim lighting? This is done for a reason. It not only produces a romantic atmosphere, but it also diverts attention away from empty seats. Adjust the lighting so that the occupied seats are highlighted to attract attention away from the unoccupied seats.

- **Custom design.** Consider having several small dining rooms located off of the main dining room. These rooms could also be used for private dining parties, celebrations or other events. The convenient thing about them is that when the restaurant is half empty; these rooms are easily closed without having to post unfriendly signs that say, "This Section Closed."

- **Presettings.** Always have the table prepared and preset before guests even see their table. It provides a nice welcoming gesture. Have the candles lit, flowers in place and wine glasses gleaming.

- **Light a candle for dessert.** If you display a dessert tray to guests, place a lit candle in the center of the tray. This provides an elegant glow around the selected desserts and sets the mood.

Attention to Detail

Never underestimate the importance of attention to detail. Let your guests know that you'll go those extra steps to make a special occasion of their dining experience. Try the following suggestions:

- **Provide purse hooks.** Mount little hooks under the bar and the tables for women to hang their purses. Sometimes there isn't a great deal of space for a woman's purse, especially at a bar.

- **Check for personal items immediately.** As soon as your guests leave the table, look in seats and under the table and chairs for possible items that may have been forgotten. You may find a simple toy, a purse or a sweater, but your customers will be very appreciative if you save them a trip before they leave the parking lot.

- **Install appropriate lighting.** Ensure that the right lights are turned on and set to the correct illumination. Most elegant restaurants and many regular restaurants are dimly lit with a combination of low lighting and burning candles. Make sure that the blinds are lowered to block out overly bright sunlight or car headlights at night. Try contacting the following companies for decorative lighting effects:

  - Candle Corporation of America, www.candlecorps.com, 800-669-6699

  - Complete Restaurant Design & Installation,www.werkheiserelectric.com, 610-938-3960

- Habitat, www.habitatweb.com, 303-443-5402, specializes in restaurant and lighting design with nationally licensed architects and interior graphic & lighting designers.

- Functional Metal, www.functionalmetal.com, 310-828-6030, manufactures all styles of decorative lighting for hotels, casinos and restaurants.

Drowning Out Operation Noises

Are guests at tables near the back being disrupted by loud noises such as banging pans and cookware, cooking, the dishwasher, etc.? In some restaurants, this type of clatter adds to the ambiance. But, in most instances, a calmer, more relaxed dining environment is preferable. Try the following:

- **Background music.** Have background music playing to drown out some of the kitchen noise. Make sure that the music is appropriate to customers' taste.

- **Plants.** Place large plants toward the back on the dining room. Objects can block some of the noise.

- **Door shields.** If the sound continues to be overbearing, consider replacing your current doors with a thicker substance to block out some of the noise. Or consider placing inexpensive carpet over the doors and possibly walls. Check with your fire code enforcement office first, however. You may have to treat the material with a fire-retardant material.

Keep Temperatures Comfortable

A combination of a hot kitchen and a room full of warm bodies, within the same building, calls for careful temperature control. Keep in mind the following basics:

- **Thermostat control.** As the temperature in a restaurant tends to be a bit warmer than the average building, keep the thermostat between 67-69° F. Adjust the temperature accordingly, until it feels right.

- **Summer-time adjustments.** In the summer when the temperature outside is hotter, you might need to lower the thermostat to 65° F to keep the air conditioning pumping at the right level.

- **Invest in the best.** If you can afford it, the best systems have a dual operating function where you can adjust the temperature settings as needed for each area of the restaurant. You can contact any heating and cooling company from your local telephone directory and order a programmable thermostat. These new systems are known for being easy to install.

- **Programmable thermostats.** Install programmable thermostats that will automatically adjust the temperature, including the heating and air conditioning systems. Also, consider installing separate controls so that unused areas can be adjusted as needed. This will not only save on your utility bill, but also make your employees and guests feel more comfortable.

- **Two nationwide heating and cooling companies**

that service restaurants are: Comfort Systems USA, www.comfortsystemsusa.com, 800-723-8431 and Sunray Heating Inc., www.sunrayheating.com, 800-734-4600.

Inviting Furniture

Take an objective look at your restaurant furniture. How comfortable and inviting does it look to customers? You want guests to linger, so give them a reason to do so – in comfort. Consider the following:

- **Hard chairs.** If you have hardback wooden chairs, consider adding color-coordinated cushions to the seat and back. This will not only add color and decoration to your dining room, but it will also give the room a cozier look.

- **Basic ergonomics.** Ensure that the seat height is appropriate to the table height. While this may vary according to the individual size of each person, try to go with the size of the average male.

- **A few places where you can order restaurant furniture are:**
  - American Chair & Seating, www.chair.com, 800-FURNITURE

  - AMI, Inc., www.arionmfg.com, 800-942-7466

  - Barstools-Inc., www.barstools-inc.com, 706-235-1670

  - Delta Furniture, www.deltafurniture.com, 514-329-1889

- Iron Furniture, www.ironfurniture.com, 800-738-4894

- Wood Seating Inc. The Restaurant Chairs Manufacturers, www.restaurant-chairs-manufacturers.com, 718-755-6216

- **Table Wobbling?** Nothing is worse than sitting at a wobbly table; it is hard to eat, distracting to talk and beverages get spilt. There are two solutions: wobble wedges and super levels. Wobble wedges are small, clear, angled leveling devices that basically take the place of all those sugar packets you see on the floor. Super levels screw into and replace the existing table feet. Both systems work great and are available at www.atlantic-pub.com, 800-541-1336, wobble wedges Item WW-01; and super levels Item SL-12.

- **A welcoming host desk.** Keep it as subtle as possible. An oversized host desk can appear somewhat intimidating. Whether remodeling or making your first selection, keep it simple. Try the following places:
  - Millwork Originals, www.millworkoriginals.com, 888-470-8666

  - Tableworks, Inc., www.tableworksinc.com, 800-214-7745

  - Restaurant Furniture Inc, www.hickory.net, 828-459-9992

Buying Carpet

Don't buy the most expensive carpet, where it will receive a lot of abuse and traffic. What good is a durable carpet four years down the road if you can't remove the stains? The reality check is the fact that you'll be replacing carpet in a few years, whether or not you want to. Here are a few tips when purchasing carpet for your restaurant:

- **Solution-dyed carpet.** Be sure to buy solution-dyed carpet. This type of carpet is ideally suited to a restaurant environment.

- **Short pile.** Don't purchase thick carpet that can harbor more dirt, dust and grime. Buy the thinner carpet that is easier to clean and vacuum on a regular basis.

- **The following companies provide carpeting:**
  - Antron, dupont.com, 800-4DUPONT.

  - Carpet Fair Commercial Division, www.carpet-faircd.com, 800-296-3247

  - Carpet One, www.allfloors.com, 305-234-3000

  - Carpet Solutions, Inc., www.millijack.com, 941-574-5394

  - Prestige Carpets, Inc., www.prestigecarpet.com, 800-887-6807

- **Nationwide carpet cleaning and restoration companies include:**
  - ChemDry, www.chemdry.com, 800-243-6379

- Milliken & Company, www.milliken.com, 800-257-3987

- Rainbow International, www.rainbowintl.com, 800-583-9100

- Servicemaster Clean, www.brant.net, 519-756-5920

- ServPro, www.servpro.com, 800-SERVPRO

Other Environmental Considerations

Once you've taken a fresh look at your interior, from the customer's point of view, turn your attention to the finer details. It can make a world of difference to the overall effect. Don't forget the following:

- **Fresh flowers and plants.** Have fresh flowers and plants in the lobby area and in the dining room. If flowers and petals start to droop, remove them. Being around a dying plant can be depressing. Using artificial plants might be an even better idea.

- **Keep roaches away.** When building or remodeling your restaurant, have roach-proof or boric acid put into the walls while they are open. This prevents cockroaches and saves on your bug bill in the long run. Where there is food, there are bugs. Contact the National Pest Management Association to find a reputable pest control company in your area. Their Web site is www.pestworld.org, or call their main office at 703-573-8330.

- **Get rid of flying pests.** A cheap, economical and safe way to get rid of them is to put red cider vinegar into a cup and mix it with a little detergent. It attracts the pesky little flies and they die. Plus, you don't have to spray your kitchen or restaurant with foul smelling bug spray.

- **Sheetrock in moisture areas.** Install sheetrock in the kitchen and bathroom areas where water and moisture are most prevalent. All sheetrock should be at least 1/2-inch thick or more, off the floor. This prevents the moisture from soaking into the bottom of the sheetrock and ruining the wall. Apply a 6-inch concrete board along the border where the floor and wall meet. This is the best method of preventing possible water damage to sheetrock walls.

Cleanliness, Tidiness and Comfort – A Few Basics You Can't Ignore

When it comes to cleanliness and tidiness, standards must never, never slip. There's nothing like cleanliness and tidiness for creating a welcoming atmosphere and a good impression. But, on a more practical note, it only takes one less-than-impressed customer to shatter your fine reputation! Consider the following basic, but important, issues:

- **Stick to a strict routine.**

- **Clean spills immediately.** Avoid the possibility of slips and falls!

- **Place chairs at empty tables where they belong - under the table.** Keep aisles clear.

- **Clear and clean all tables as soon as customers**

have vacated them. This applies even if no one is currently waiting for a table.

- **Create an impression of orderliness.** Ensure that wrapped silverware and table fixtures are in place.

- **Aromas and odors.** Keep trash well away from the dining area.

- **Spills on carpets.** Avoid the possibility of lingering ugly odors. Clean and shampoo any spills, immediately, before the stain and smell become too difficult to remove.

- **Scented candles.** Try making the atmosphere more pleasant by burning scented candles at each table. Another option you could try is to use the Smelleze Restaurant/Bar Deodorizer pouch. Order it from www.no-odor.com. It cleanses the air by absorbing and neutralizing unpleasant odors and works in an area of up to 400 square feet.

- **Ventilation.** Install a ventilation system that is powerful enough to cope with the demands of your restaurant. Don't forget that the aroma of a grilled steak can make a customer's mouth water, but the smell of a burnt steak can have the opposite affect!

- **Provide a cleaning checklist**. Create a cleaning checklist for each shift. Include the date, time and specific personnel and their duties. Some people know they should do certain duties, but they won't put the extra effort in without you spelling it out for them. Make sure each individual knows the tasks they are to perform and the standards required of them.

Clean, Presentable Restrooms

Don't become so obsessed with the dining room area that you forget the restrooms. Nothing is worse than walking into a foul-smelling bathroom with toilet paper and paper towels everywhere! Apart from the obvious, insist on the following:

- **Assign the bathrooms to two employees every shift**. Stick to a strict rotation from one employee to the next. Ensure that the toilets are clean and wiped down properly, during and after every shift.

- **Clean up splashed water on the sink counters and from the floor**. Wipe off soap drippings. Again, this procedure should be performed during and after every shift.

- **Keep a can of air freshener for customers in each stall.** Place some potpourri and/or scented candles on the counters.

- **Clean the mirrors as needed.**

- **Never, ever run out.** Ensure a proper supply of toilet paper, soap and paper towels.

Give your guests a reason for wanting to come back.

THE EXTRA MILE

Food and Entertainment

People usually dine out for more than just the food. Reward guests for choosing you rather than your competitors. Give them a reason for wanting to come back. That means you need to exceed expectations. Here's how it's done:

- **Help guest's party.** When a group is dining out to celebrate a birthday or an anniversary, get the staff together and sing "Happy Birthday" to them. Offer a free complimentary dessert for the birthday person or couple having the anniversary. For an anniversary, you could have someone from the restaurant, maybe a manager or yourself, dedicate a toast to their long years of marriage and many more years of happiness to come.

- **Take pictures.** If you notice a guest with a camera, offer to take pictures for them. That way everyone there can be in the photo. Be sure to find out exactly how to operate the camera. Most likely, they will appreciate the extra effort you have taken to help them preserve a special memory.

- **Keep cameras on hand.** Keep a Polaroid camera at each station to help guests preserve those special memories. Old friends are always getting together and dining out - and often they forget to bring a camera along. Imagine their surprise when you pull out your trusty Polaroid. Go a step further and have pre-made picture frames with your restaurant name and phone number. These picture frames need not be expensive. Try www.ueco.ab.ca/Frames/paper-frames1.htm for a start. Every time they look at their picture, they'll think of your establishment.

- **Honor your guests.** Designate a place on the wall where you honor your regular guests. Make an event out of it. Choose a quiet time. Devote your attention, exclusively, to these regulars and invite them to bring their friends along. Take pictures and post them on the wall. Offer them a complimentary dessert or drink.

Expand Your Services

One of the best ways to attract customers (new and old) is to expand your range of current services. You can do this by offering new menu items, as well as more of a selection of the types of menu items already offered. Here are a few ideas:

- **More alcohol-free alternatives.** Offer more than simple coffee with sugar and cream; invest in an espresso machine and offer customers a wide selection of high-quality beans. Grind the beans freshly each time.

- **Tea can be more than just tea.** Offer decaf, herbal and hot tea, as well as iced tea. Provide both unsweetened and sweetened tea.

- **Different juice options**. Have a variety of juices to

choose from so that you can increase sales from those customers that would normally opt for water as opposed to sodas, coffee, tea or wine beverages. Many parents don't want their children drinking sodas and tea.

- **Vegetarian meals.** More and more people are turning away from meat. Ensure that you grasp this segment of the market by offering a good selection of meat-free meals.

- **Banquet and private parties.** If you have the space available, begin by catering wedding banquets on Saturdays, between the hours of 10 a.m. and 4 p.m. You'll be exchanging a Saturday of uncertain business at various rates for a Saturday of guaranteed business at a fixed price and menu.

- **Menus in Braille.** Have a few menus translated and produced in Braille. This is a simple service that most restaurants don't think about. Impress your customers by being equipped for everyone who visits your restaurant. See www.quikscrybe.com, www.duxburysystems.com or www.access2020.com.

- **Bilingual menu.** Go the extra mile and have a few menus translated and produced in other languages. Start by translating the most common spoken non-English language in your geographic region.

Handling Customer Complaints

Despite all our efforts to the contrary, things do sometimes go horribly wrong. We have to handle it as best as we can. If you are realistic enough to acknowledge this fact, then you have the ability to be one step ahead of your competitors - simply by being prepared. There are, however, certain "damage limitation" measures that you can take to preserve your untarnished reputation:

- **Don't keep a customer waiting.** The instant you hear a customer complaining, drop what you're doing. Go immediately to the customer who is making the complaint. Don't keep an already agitated individual waiting a moment longer than is necessary. They want their issue resolved - NOW! Your goal is to keep matters from escalating and getting out of hand.

- **Stay calm and objective.** Approach the customer with a warm smile and a genuine openness. Politely ask them to explain the issue and listen to them as intently as possible. Don't try to argue with them or to explain the other person's viewpoint. When a customer is already angry and upset, they don't care. Likewise, they care less about your policies and procedures. If they want something that goes against your regular policy, say something like, "Well, normally that isn't our policy, but I will make an exception." That may be all they want to hear.

- **Apologize no matter what.** Even if you believe the customer is being irate and ridiculous, apologize. It doesn't matter who is REALLY wrong. At this point, it is your job to make this customer happy, once again. You've got to appease them. Tell them you're sorry, because that is what they want to hear. Then ask them how they would prefer you to resolve the problem. Simply ask them what they want you do to, but be sure to phrase the question in a way that won't sound condescending or sarcastic. For instance, don't say, "Well, what would you have me do?" Instead, say something like, "I'm really sorry. How best could I make it up to you?"

- **Take immediate action.** If possible, immediately remove whoever or whatever caused the problem. Exceed their expectations by not only fixing the problem, but also offering them something more. Don't stop until they seem satisfied and overwhelmed by your efforts.

- **Thank them for bringing the issue to your attention.** Let them know that it helps you to be more efficient when you are aware of issues that need attention. After they leave your restaurant, be sure to follow up with a personal phone call or a handwritten note the next day.

Turn Negatives into Positives

There will always be situations that happen beyond your control, but they don't have to turn into disasters. Turn a negative issue into a positive alternative. Here's how:

- **Suggest other options.** When items sell out, offer other alternatives to your guests so they aren't sitting there wondering what to choose next.

- **Smile, accidents happen.** When spills and messy accidents happen, smile and clean it up as quickly as possible. Show more concern for the customer experiencing the embarrassment than the mess. Reassure them that it's okay and that it isn't a problem. Offer to replace drink and food if necessary.

- **Resolve problems quickly.** If a guest expresses any kind of displeasure, immediately focus on how to make them happy again

- **Open lines of communication.** Establish a toll-free number for customers to call and leave feedback. This allows customers to make a formal complaint to someone other than the person that they perceive to have caused the problem.

- **Freebies for waiting.** When guests have to wait to be seated, offer them something to entice them to stay. Offer them a free beverage, peanuts, bread sticks or something else that's simple and easy to serve.

- **Guests who arrive at closing.** Politely inform them that the restaurant is closing, but you will do everything in your power to see that they have an enjoyable meal. Serve them promptly, but not in obvious haste. Concentrate on the closing tasks you can do without interrupting your late guests; ignore the ones you cannot do while they're still there. In other words, don't dim the lights on them, cut off the background music, vacuum or stack up empty chairs around them. Remember, closing time is when you stop seating guests, it is not the time you actually stop serving guests.

Offer a Fast Lunch

A fast lunch is one of the best ways to maximize profits:

- **Hang up a sign that guarantees a fast lunch in fifteen minutes** - or its free.

- **Stop-watches.** Buy cheap stop-watches at Wal-mart or Target. Place them at each table. Prove that you mean what you say! Have the waiter or waitress set the timer as soon as orders are taken.

- **Be selective.** Make sure you limit the program to certain menu items that can be prepared in the time frame you've set.

- **Restrict the offer to small parties** under a specific number of individuals.

- **Provisos about add-ons.** For example, make it quite clear that you may need to adjust the time when appetizers are ordered.

- **Make sure that you have extra staff to cover lunch hours.** Lunch hours are critical, as employees must get back to work by a certain time. But remember, if you do it well, your program will definitely gain attention and increase your lunch sales enough to offset a few free lunches.

Provide "Add-Ons" and Specialty Items

Add-on options, where a customer might receive an additional side item for a small additional price, greatly increase your overall sales volume. Branded items, likewise, offer great opportunities for maximizing profits. Bear in mind the following:

- **Promote add-ons.** Encourage servers to offer them to customers when they are placing their orders. For example, some dishes are served with a side salad or bread sticks, but others are not. Offer a side salad for $1.99 extra when a customer is ordering a dish that has no additional side orders with it. If you sell a total of 100 side salads a day, that's an additional gross sale of $199 or $72,635 per year.

- **Develop a signature item.** Choosing a signature item from your menu takes planning and preparation.

- **Brand your menu items.** Promoting brand named ingredients in items can increase your profits by as much as 20 percent! Often a brand name is synonymous with quality. Doesn't a layer of Grey Poupon™ Dijon Mustard sound much more enticing than simply stating a layer of mustard?

- **Provide feature items everyday.** It keeps your regulars from getting bored with your menu, while keeping you and your staff innovative and constantly creating new and exciting meals. It also gives you a chance to promote low-cost menu items and increase sales of those particular items.

- **Create a signature dessert.** Every dessert menu needs a signature dessert. The idea is to have people craving one of your desserts just at thought of it. Display the unique aspects of each dessert item through photos, or on a dessert tray that you display right at the table. It's hard for people to ignore dessert if it's right in front of them.

- **Create signature icons.** Place a miniature "icon"

beside the signature item you want to promote on your menu. This is an immediate indication to your guests that this item is special and receives extra attention in preparation as your establishment takes pride in its success and popularity.

Provide Consistently Excellent Service

It's no secret that if a guest returns twice in a month as opposed to their once-a-month visit, then you've just doubled your sales. This is the best way to increase sales. All you have to do is provide consistent excellent service in every facet of your restaurant. Customers need to know that they can rely on your service. Review all aspects of your restaurant, from external appearance to employee attentiveness and the quality of the food you serve up to your guests. Take an overview:

- **Consistency is the key.** Ensure that standards of service never slip. If customers visit one day and everything is perfect, but the next visit provides a disastrous experience, your credibility is undermined.

- **Be flexible.** While it is necessary to have a measure of control, you also need to be flexible. Changes are always taking place in the food and beverage business and organizational goals continue to evolve. As new technology develops, new ways of doing things will affect how procedures are used in your restaurant. Adapt to these changes without interrupting the quality of the flow and service to the guests.

Motivate your staff to sell.

CHAPTER EIGHT

EMPLOYEES

Your Staff is Your Best Selling and Cost-Cutting Resource

Your waitstaff, bartenders and cocktail waiters are your sales people. They are the ones actually talking to your guests. So the greater their knowledge-based selling skills, the more money your restaurant will make. Surely, you've been to a restaurant where the waitstaff described the special for the day, or one of the establishment's delightful desserts. Did it sound too good to pass up? Try the following approach:

- **Use selling skills at the table.** People are apprehensive about trying out something new. The more that your waitstaff knows about the meals on the core menus and the specials being offered, the more direct sales they can make right at the table.

- **Provide a selling environment.** Create an atmosphere with detailed, informative menus. Before the restaurant opens or changes shifts, hold a pre-shift sales briefing. Give your waitstaff ideas on how to sell to the customers, how to make the food sound more appealing and tasty. Take the time to teach and train them appropriately and your sales will climb.

- **Motivate your staff to sell.** During the brief meeting, provide structured and organized agendas that your waitstaff can easily follow at the highlight of a busy day. Give them a pep talk and take the time to introduce new items thoroughly. Work with them on the pronunciation of the menu items to increase their comfort and confidence level.

- **Include the kitchen staff.** Have your kitchen staff describe to your waitstaff how the food is prepared, the unique ingredients involved. If the kitchen staff can have the mouths of your waitstaff watering for tasty food by the end of the briefing, imagine how motivated they'll be to sell these same ideas to the guests they'll be serving!

- **As a manager, smile and greet your employees.** Treat your employees with the same respect as you do your guests. Smile and greet them each morning. Don't act as if their paycheck at the end of the week is a substitute for your professionalism - it isn't. Show them how much you appreciate them. When they give you a great idea, reward them with some extra time off, an up-front parking place, a ribbon to wear on their uniform. There are numerous ways to recognize your employees for great work, but also recognize them for upbeat personalities and their willingness to share great ideas.

Practical Training Strategies

Training, in the restaurant trade, is never an easy task. Each employee has different needs, learning abilities, skills, talent, goals, sometimes language barriers, etc. Even allowing for these differences, there are a few tried-and-tested approaches you can take that will really work for your establishment. Try the following:

- **Orientation should be conducted by top-level management.** Make sure that new employees learn the rules and regulations correctly from the start. Tenured employees are more likely to share shortcuts and simple things they can get away with. Also, by having someone of importance within the company spending quality time orientating them, new employees feel more appreciated and valued.

- **Use scripts and role-play.** Practice greeting guests through role-playing with other employees pretending to be guests. For a telephone greeting, you could have them practice a short script or phrase by repeating it aloud several times. Allow your staff enough freedom to express the idea you are training them to convey until it feels natural to them. You don't want their words to sound rehearsed, or their actions to look like mechanical robots. Nothing is worse than sounding fake or insincere. Atlantic Publishing sells The Hospitality Role Playing Kit, one for the dining room staff and one for alcoholic beverage service staff. Visit www.atlantic-pub.com for the details.

- **Utilize the right trainers.** Ask for volunteers. Some employees don't want to train someone else. Usually, they aren't rewarded for the extra effort and it takes time away from their own progress and tip money. So, offer them a bonus for this training time. There's nothing wrong with a little incentive. Consult your staff and ask their opinions about who was the best at helping them when they started. Some people are natural trainers and enjoy training.

- **Share your profit and loss information during**

training sessions. Staff will immediately feel involved. Background knowledge is a great motivator. Open up and share with your employees the awful facts about owning and operating a business. People who have never owned or managed any type of business have some strange misconceptions about profits. Educate them on the facts and they might come up with ideas on how to increase your profits.

- **Hang laminated photos in the kitchen.** Guests expect their plates to match the exact photo on display in a menu or a brochure advertisement; help your chefs and servers by hanging the same photos in the kitchen. Provide a photo album of each item so that a new chef or server will have a point of reference.

- **Provide basic kitchen training to servers.** Offer instructions about the quality of ingredients, preparation procedures and the cooking techniques used in your restaurant. Give them written training materials such as a manual or notebook for quick reference. Provide accurate descriptions of how different items are prepared and taste. Invite staff to taste different foods. Have the waitstaff work in the kitchen or preparation once a month or initially in the training period. They will learn a lot about the food quality and ingredients.

- **Delegating means more profits.** Cross-train your employees to replace each other and help out in other areas. All staff should be able to answer customer questions and serve guests if necessary, even if it isn't their regular job. People get sick, go on vacation and leave unexpectedly. Someone else should always be able to fill his or her role temporarily.

- **Ensure proper training time.** Some employees will learn a new skill the first time you show them, while others need to be shown again and again. Therefore, the best way to train is daily for half-hour to one-hour training sessions. Use as many elements of visual, auditory and interactive role-playing as possible.

- **Training is an on-going necessary activity.** Your training sessions aren't over once you've trained a new employee well enough to do their job. Lead your staff in training sessions for continual growth and development. Use books, posters and training video tapes. A great resource for all of these tools is www.atlantic-pub.com.

- **Learn from competitors.** Visit your competitors and learn from them. Think of it as training and learning. Ideas catch on from one business to another and it happens all the time. Make the idea yours by building and expanding upon it.

- **Training seminars and workshops.** Off-site training sessions are great for developing ideas. Listen to training and motivational tapes. Read similar books, including the business press. Don't be afraid to try new and different things.

Proper Conduct

There are a few universally accepted "dos and don'ts" when it comes to staff behavior. For example, your employees should know not to congregate in groups and carry on personal conversations around guests. Smoking shouldn't be allowed. Bad language, arguing or yelling in the kitchen that can be heard above noises should not be tolerated. Always, always, be courteous and smile! Other general considerations include:

- **Handling money.** It's rude to count out change or write out checks in front of guests, or jingle coins and pull out wadded bills. Instruct your staff to take payments to the cash register or to their station. They should bring back the proper change with enough for a tip. For example, don't bring back ten single dollar bills.

- **Handling menus.** Instruct staff to carry the menus in their hands, not under their arms or in a belt loop. Servers should then wait until guests are seated before placing the menu in front of each individual, front side up and in the correct orientation. In general, don't hand guests the menu immediately, unless they specifically reach for it.

- **Be efficient, but not rushed.** When leading guests to their table, don't walk so far ahead of them that you leave them behind. This might make customers feel rushed and uncomfortable. While it is imperative to be efficient, never hasten your guests along.

Written Job Descriptions

If you don't have detailed, written job descriptions for yourself and every single person in your restaurant, you need to write them as soon as possible. Here are a few general guidelines:

- **Take your time writing these descriptions.** Include every single task and responsibility.

- **What to include in a job description.** Try to be as specific as possible while keeping the length around one to two pages. List each specific task to be completed as well as the desired end result. Include job requirements of the individual's physical capabilities, such as being able to lift at least 30 pounds. Also, include any necessary pre-requisites such as level of education and skills. Usually there is a signature line for both the employee and the manager indicating that the manager has gone over the job description with the employee.

- **Hand out a copy of the job description to new and potential employees.** It can act as a checklist, in case you forgot to discuss a particular issue, during the interview.

- **Start a written description for the position that has the highest turnover rate.** Involve your employees. Get them to check for omissions. After all, you don't do their job everyday and might not realize exactly what's involved.

- **Remember, the responsibilities of a job can't be determined as you go along.** Working this way without direction is very frustrating and the fastest way to lose your best employees.

- **Revise job descriptions on a regular basis.** An old, outdated job description is just as useless as not having one. Over time, people, industries and expectations change and so do jobs. Update job descriptions at least every year, more often if there are changes to policies, strategies and procedures. You may even decide to change a job description because the current individual has raised the standards of that position. The next individual who replaces them will need to be of a similar standard.

- **Use the computer.** Basic templates for job descriptions and employee handbooks may be found at www.atlantic-pub.com.

Hiring Strategies

Knowing exactly who to hire is never easy. It takes commitment to interview, effectively asking the right (and legal) questions and really listening to the answers. An astute interviewer also needs to be aware of what potential employees are not saying or are hesitant to admit. The signs of good and bad employees are there before we hire them. The problem is that we often wait until we are in desperate need before we start the hiring process. Use the following tips as a guideline to streamline your hiring procedures:

- **You can't get to know an individual through an application.** The application should only be used as a question buffer.

- **Don't spend as much time reading applications and resumés as you do interviewing.** If you choose the best application with the best wording and spelling, you might be short-changing yourself. Sometimes, people with excellent written communication and higher degrees are less likely to be serious about a new job in your restaurant. Most likely, they're simply passing through, waiting for a better offer elsewhere. If you don't want the hassle of rehiring and retraining someone else in six weeks, meet as many of the applicants in person as possible. Your intuition and gut instinct will tell you more about them than their written application will.

- **Recruit staff that has an interest in the food service industry.** Go to food service programs held by local colleges and trade schools. Take the time to speak to instructors and students regarding the potential opportunities at your restaurant. Discuss the benefits of your training program. While visiting these places, leave flyers and brochures on their bulletin boards, as well as at gourmet shops and other food businesses. Even if their intended stay is brief, hire students for part-time work and work out internship programs. Their excitement about the business may be catching and invigorating to the rest of your staff.

- The following companies are recruiting organizations for the food service and restaurant industry:
  - Agri-Tech Personnel, Inc., www.agri-techpersonnel.com

  - Chef Jobs Network, www.chefjobsnetwork.com

  - Food Headhunters, www.foodheadhunters.com

  - Food Management Search, www.foodmanagementsearch.com

  - Kinsa Group, www.kinsa.com

  - Mixtec Group, www.mixtec.net

  - Professional Search and Recruiting,

www.psrecruit.com
- Resources in Food, www.rifood.com

- Restaurant Manager,
  www.restaurantmanager.net

It's All In the Attitude

The more upbeat and motivated your employees, the more successful they will be with customers. If the staff has a positive attitude, it will reflect upon your establishment and radiate a welcoming atmosphere. The result is a fun, relaxing environment where sales flourish along with your profits. Try to achieve the following:

- **Boost motivation.** Use intangible incentives to boost motivation in your employees. Praise them when they perform well. Show them you appreciate them. It isn't very motivating when your boss only appears to see the mistakes and never the accomplishments.

- **Delegate.** It reduces stress on yourself; it also boosts your employees' self-worth and commitment. Let them in on the decision-making process and you might be surprised at their abilities. It adds more meaning and value to their jobs.

- **Laugh and encourage laughter on the job.** Just because employees are enjoying themselves doesn't mean they are neglecting their jobs. Too serious a business can induce an uncomfortable environment and increase employee turnover, simply because people aren't happy. No matter how much you can afford to pay your employees, money doesn't buy happiness.

- **Smile.** A genuine smile can speak volumes to a customer – much more than any rehearsed script. Guests want to feel special. A nice smile can do that. However, when employing staff, remember that a sincere smile is one thing you can't teach to employees. They either have it or they don't. You can, however, expect your waitstaff to use direct eye contact and smile when approaching customers.

- **Insist that your employees treat kids like people too.** Ask them to go out of their way to talk to children. Give them their own menu and offer crayons or some small toy to occupy their attention while their parents are trying to decide what to choose from the menu. If they are old enough, ask them what they want to eat. Parents appreciate people who take time with their kids.

- **Make it a house rule that servers speak to your guests in complete sentences - not phrases.** Using phrases such as, "Smoking or non?" or "More tea?" gives guests the impression that the staff is in a hurry and they're being treated like just another customer. "Would you prefer smoking or non-smoking?" Which one sounds less rushed and more polite to you? Insist that servers take time to talk to your valued customers.

- **Make the front-of-the-house responsible for assisting customers with their coats.** Hand gentlemen their coats; hold coats up for the ladies, especially the elderly. Hand children's coats to their parents. Stand out from the crowd. The sad fact is that few restaurants provide this type of courtesy anymore.

- **Make diners feel important.** Encourage your staff to remember names and favorite drinks of your regular customers. Managers and owners should try to visit tables whenever possible to greet customers and simply talk to them. What good is it if customers only see the manager or owner whenever there is a problem?

- **Handling difficult customers.** Advise your employees to concentrate on the positive aspects of an individual's personality, appearance and behavior. It usually works! This is the secret of being on your best behavior in less-than-favorable circumstances or company. If a customer is rude without reasonable cause, simply instruct your staff to ignore and forget about it and concentrate instead on the great customers you have had that day, especially the ones that really made you smile.

- **Encourage employees to give compliments to your guests.** A compliment is one way of letting customers know that you're paying attention. But, only do so if it's genuinely meant.

Managing Employees and Coworkers

No matter what kind of policies you have in place or how good the quality of your product, if your employees are not performing and unmanageable, your business will suffer as a result. Concentrate on ways to modify their behavior more positively, rather than criticizing them, yelling at them or reprimanding them in ways that may hurt their self-esteem or aggravate the situation even further. Too much criticism may make people bitter and vengeful to the point that they purposely sabotage your efforts. Give no one a reason to feel this way or act in this manner. Take the following approach:

- **Pass on positives.** If you hear guests complimenting the food, pass this good news on to the cooks. They are in the back and rarely have a chance to interact with guests. Let them know that their efforts are being appreciated.

- **Capitalize on ideas from your staff.** While it is necessary to maintain and adhere to standard recipes, let your staff help you create those recipes. Remember, your servers are the direct link communicating with your guests. They hear the comments and suggestions and have to answer all the questions. Listen to your staff's ideas; allow them to expound and create wonderful selections. It will also give them a sense of accomplishment, of belonging and self-worth. In the long run, you can't lose.

- **Give your staff a change of scenery.** Round everyone up, or if this is impractical, give out gift certificates to a restaurant where they can be served for a change. Think of it as a field trip. This gets everyone away from the pressures of business and allows them to loosen up and enjoy their creativity. Talk to them about their thoughts on the restaurant. Ask them for ideas regarding areas that need change, updates and/or additions either to the menu, the food preparation or business in general. Sometimes a meeting such as this away from the work environment can create a lot more progress than any other meetings before or after work.

- **Meet employees' expectations.** Be aware that your employees will treat your customers with the same respect as you treat them. If your employees feel that you are behaving in your own interest rather than theirs, then they'll take care of business as usual. In other words, they'll only do what's required of them and nothing beyond. However, if your employees truly believe you're acting on their behalf, they will go above and beyond your expectations.

- **Treat employees as individuals.** Everyone is different with different goals, ideals and perceptions. For this reason alone, you cannot treat all your employees exactly alike. (But, this doesn't mean you shouldn't use the same disciplinary actions for bad behavior!) For instance, what might motivate and influence one employee might not make much of a difference to another employee. Talk to each individual in order to discover his or her likes and dislikes, thoughts and perceptions, goals and aspirations. Only then can you begin treating them as individuals.

- **Manage absenteeism and tardiness.** Ensure that you have a written policy that spells out what you will tolerate and what you won't tolerate. Give this written policy to each employee when they are first hired. Post a copy by the time clock as an occasional reminder.

- **Consistency.** Believe it or not, the problem that most employees have with managers is inconsistent policies. In other words, treat everyone the same. That means no favorite employees, no scapegoats and absolutely no selective memory. Get your facts straight. Write down all behavioral problems, including how you handle the situation so that you have something to refer back to later if the problem ever occurs again with a different employee.

- **Let employees set goals.** Allow employees to help you set goals. Most people want their own ideas and suggestions to be a proven success. Therefore, they will do everything in their power to see that it happens. If the goal comes from you, it was your idea and it soon becomes your problem. As a manager, you are now in the position of motivating your employees to achieve your goals. By allowing employees to create their own goals, you're side-stepping the whole "it's not my job" issue.

Set Standards of Staff Performance

Your perception of a job and your employee's perception of the same job could be two completely different ideals. To overcome this problem, set clear standards of performance so that employees know exactly what to do and how well to do it. Consider the following issues:

- **Lead by example.** Communicate clearly and lead staff by example. For instance, the way in which you attend to guests' special requests or questions about items on the menu will not go unnoticed.

- **Make sure that your expectations are realistic and possible to achieve.** There's no quicker way to frustrate and lose employees than to set unrealistic goals and impossible standards that are unachievable.

- **Give real feedback.** Staff need and want to know how well they're doing. Don't wait until a 6-month or yearly review to give your employees feedback on their performance. Unless you've taken exceptional notes, you aren't going to be able to remember much past the most recent experiences. They deserve feedback for more than what happened last week. Give feedback on a daily basis. All it takes is a quick pat on the back. "I heard how you handled that customer's request for a different drink. Good job!" Don't hesitate to tell employees how well they're doing in front of others. It makes them feel good and is great positive reinforcement. On the other hand, address poor behavior immediately so that there's no question of favoritism. Try to handle all criticism and negative feedback in private.

- **Timing of performance appraisals.** It's best to give performance appraisals on a quarterly basis, or at least twice a year. It motivates your employees and opens the lines of communication. If employees are only evaluated once a year, they get no second chance to redeem themselves for another year. By then they've most likely grown frustrated and quit, putting you back into the training mode. In the long run, continuous training costs you money.

- **Conducting performance appraisals.** Be prepared. That means taking notes year round on employees' job performances, both positive and negative. Accentuate the positives as much as possible and when you need to discuss a negative issue, be sure to criticize the performance, not the person. Help the employee find solutions. Record all comments in writing and have the employee sign the appraisal as well as including your own signature.

• **Conduct exit interviews.** If you have a great employee leaving, conduct an exit interview to find out more. Be open minded, as the problem could even be you. If so, try to deal with it as best as you can. Correct the problem immediately so that you do not continue to lose other good employees. Good employees are hard to find and even harder to keep. Don't let them get away because of something that could be corrected or changed.

Impressive Uniforms

The uniforms worn by your staff project the image of your restaurant. Take a good look at the appearance of each employee. Decide whether they reflect your restaurant's style. If you want your employees' uniforms to look impressive, attend to the following details:

• **Colors can alter reality.** Have your uniforms made in solid colors that are generally appropriate for most people's color tone, for example, navy or teal. You want your staff looking energetic and as if they are glowing as they bounce around from one table to the next. Colors that conflict with their personal color scheme will make them look dull, shabby, weary and unhealthy.

• **Ensure an appropriate fit.** Ensure that your employees are wearing the proper size for their physique. Making do with what you have available simply won't do. If you give the impression that you don't care about the appearance of your staff, then you might also be giving guests the impression that you don't care about your business. Try the following companies for great-looking uniforms: Chefwear at www.chefwear.com, 800-568-2433; Chef Revival at www.chefrevival.com, 800-352-2433; Gourmet Gear at www.gourmetgear.com, 800-682-4635; Culinary Classics at www.culinaryclassics.com, 877-378-4855; or UniVogue at www.univogue.com, 800-527-3374.

• **Accessorize and individualize.** While you may require restaurant staff to wear specific uniforms and have a few ground rules for appearance, do allow your employees to wear discreet accessories that will give them their individuality. This allows them the freedom to make some choices in their attire and helps them to project a more positive image to their customers, as well as to feel self-assured in their appearance.

• **Name tags.** Have your employees wear name tags, including the managers. Although, a server may have told a group of people at a table his or her name, guests aren't likely to remember it fifteen minutes later, when they need something. Often, guests feel embarrassed or uncomfortable when they need their waitress or waiter and can't recall their name. Unlike being verbally told, seeing a name written on a name tag is easier for more people to remember. You can order name tags from All Star Nametags at www.allstarnametags.com, 800-852-1294; Custom Names & Signs at www.customnames.com, 210-737-3200; or Custom Stamp and Engraving Ltd. at www.rstamp.com,   250-383-6171.

CHAPTER NINE

MARKETING FOR PROFITABILITY

The Real Value of Marketing - Spend Your Money Where it Counts!

Marketing isn't a one-time campaign to get your business up and running. What many companies fail to realize is that marketing is an on-going campaign.

- **Forward planning.** As soon as one marketing expedition is over, have a plan and a strategy in place for the next marketing venture. It's the surest way of gaining new customers.

- **Use your marketing budget to target areas in the same vicinity as your restaurant.** People are more likely to drive 3-5 miles to a convenient, familiar area to try a new restaurant than 8-10 miles out of their way to an unfamiliar environment.

- **Take advantage of cross-promotion.** Often, you can team up with retailers, entertainment companies, clubs and organizations to promote an event or a special offer that may directly or indirectly promote your restaurant. For instance, you could offer all skaters at a local skating rink a free dessert during a particular weekend.

- **Promote through community events.** Community events such as fund-raisers, parades, carnivals and festivals provide excellent opportunities to promote your restaurant. Become involved and participate where possible. You'll be surprised at how well such simple techniques like these can enhance your business and name recognition.

- **Be a community role model.** Whenever disaster strikes in your neighborhood, be available to assist in whatever way possible. Food, ice, fresh water. People will remember that more than any whole-page ad you could take out in a local newspaper.

Develop a Unique Selling Position

Every business needs a unique selling position. Sell the part of your business that is different from everyone else's. It can be the fact that you have exceptional desserts, an outstanding signature item and the only seafood restaurant on your side of town or free appetizers. Choose the points you want to sell and use them as a slogan with your logo. Also, try the following suggestions:

- **Use "niche" marketing tactics.** Decide on a factor or aspect of your business that is better than all the rest. Promote that idea at every opportunity that you get. It could be that you are known for the best Southern food, or that you're the only family entertainment restaurant with fun and activities for the whole family. Other ideas are that you could provide the best home-cooked meals in your region. How about becoming the health spot for people wanting a broad selection without sacrificing good taste.

- **Initiate "four walls" marketing.** Begin your

marketing campaign by marketing your business right inside the walls of your restaurant. Set up easel posters, suggestion boxes and decals in the lobby area. Include noticeable register toppers and brochures at the checkout counter. Hang posters of signature drinks in the bar area. The dining room is your best marketing area, as customers spend most of their time here. Post special boards, provide tabletop displays and specialty menus such as water, beer, specialty desserts and, of course, a wine list.

Build A Web Site

Today, every restaurant needs a Web site. You want them to find you, not your competitors. The following tips offer a few important "musts" when creating a Web site:

- **Photos.** Upload mouth-watering pictures of your signature items and other great-tasting dishes.

- **Be sure to have a contact page with your phone number and e-mail address.** Provide a map with written directions on how to find your restaurant. Provide a link where customers can type in their address and receive printed directions.

- **Gizmo Graphics Web Design,** www.gizwebs.com. A professional Web design company utilizing the latest technology. Gizmo Graphics offers low-cost, high-quality Web design services catering to the food service industry.

- **Monitor your Web site traffic.** Monitor your Web site traffic through such services as www.sitemeter.com. This way you can tell from where the majority of your traffic is coming, whether by search engines or through other links and affiliates. Most importantly, you'll know which affiliate links are worth paying for (and which ones aren't).

Other Online Marketing Opportunities

Build on the power of your Web site. Create an interactive Web site where you can communicate with your customers and they can communicate with you. Allow them to e-mail questions and you post the answers. Post a recipe of the day. Create trivia questions and offer little rewards and surprises. Encourage your visitors to participate:

- **Affiliate links.** Try to establish affiliate links to other operations similar to yours, as well as your vendors and local cinema and entertainment sites. Also consider linking with other food service organizations, nutrition sites and food and beverage-related industry businesses. Join other online restaurant communities and post your expert advice. People will appreciate your help, as well as come to know your name and your restaurant. It's free self-promotion and an excellent avenue by which to spread the word about your business.

- **A few online restaurant communities you could check out are:**
  - www.atlantic-pub.com
  - www.chefnet.com
  - www.food.com
  - www.foodnet.com
  - www.nmrestaurants.com

- www.restaurantchat.com
- www.therestaurantgame.com
- www.webfoodpros.com

- **Create an online community.** Invite your chef to participate in sharing his culinary expertise. Provide a forum where other restaurant business-people can discuss the industry, post questions and exchange advice.

- **Create an online newsletter.** It's hard to find a Web site that doesn't have its own newsletter. Increase your reputation and awareness of your own business. The best part is it costs nothing to send 10 or 10,000,000 e-mail newsletters. Include good and interesting content but, of course, promote the restaurant. For example, you could produce a newsletter on the new arrival of the Beaujolais Villages wines from France, its history, etc., and promote the "Beaujolais Villages Night on Wednesday" at your restaurant.

- **Send online press releases.** Share culinary news-breaking information with the rest of the world. Send a press release through online services as opposed to the traditional methods of postal mail. This way you have a better chance of reaching more people at a significantly lower cost.

Traditional Marketing Techniques

In your search for innovative advertising methods, don't overlook the more traditional approach. It is, after all, "tried and tested" in the restaurant promotion market. Consider the following techniques:

- **Highway billboards.** If you are located just off of a major highway, you will definitely want to consider investing in a billboard sign along the highway. This will attract the traveling public passing by.

- **Use radio broadcast advertising.** Radio advertising has several advantages. It costs less to reach a higher percentage of potential guests over newspaper advertising. The lower costs allow for more frequent broadcasts. Radio is also one of the most effective media at instantly getting people to recognize and maintain a slogan message.

- **Newspaper advertising.** When choosing a newspaper in which to advertise, you must consider the circulation size, locality, ad size and rates.

- **Advertise at movie theaters.** Most cinemas now feature revolving screen advertisements before the actual movie previews begin. These are great for local advertisements, as they're shown several times in rotation.

- **TV advertising.** Don't forget about special TV advertising. Select a local cable TV station or advertise on a appropriate cooking channel.

Other Innovative Marketing Techniques

Apart from the tried-and-tested marketing techniques, you may wish to branch out and try the following:

- **Donate edible leftovers.** Restaurants often have edible leftover food at the end of each day. Several food banks in your local area could pick up the food and transport it to where it's needed the most.

- **Outdoor display.** Invest in an eye-catching outdoor display. Locate it above your restaurant for maximum impact. Place a classic car, airplane, inflatable giant monster or hot air balloon.

- **Include surprises in carryout orders.** For every carry out order, include a little pleasant surprise gift such as a piece of candy, a thank-you note, a discount coupon or some other nice goodie. People will appreciate the thoughtfulness.

- **Write free articles.** Consider writing free articles for restaurant and food industry-related e-zines and printed magazines. Many of the editors would love to receive an article from someone with experience in the field. Often, the editor will include a short bio about the author at the end of the article.

- **Offer a bed & breakfast combo.** While you may not be a Bed & Breakfast Inn, if there is a hotel near you, try to team up together. Whenever they have special conferences that might bring in a thousand or more guests, offer some free breakfast incentives to the hotel's conference-goers.

- **Team up with local hotels.** Promote an affiliate program with hotels in your area. The idea is that you provide something for them in return for them distributing your brochures, providing a slot for your restaurant in their informational channel, etc.

- **Press kits.** Put together a press kit containing sales letters, brochures, a menu sample, news clippings, business cards, etc. Send it to the local chamber of commerce.

- **Share your knowledge.** Share your knowledge with others and earn respect and recognition for your business. Achieve this through part-time classes at a local college, trade school or cooking classes in the restaurant.

Get to Know Your Customers

Spend a couple of weeks gathering information from customers at each meal. Try to choose a time that doesn't involve a holiday or a local community event that might bring in a lot of non-locals. Try the following tips:

- **Use the guest book.** Ask your patrons to fill out the guest book. Collect such information as birth dates and anniversaries. Have an employee transfer the information into a computer database system to use as a mailing list to send promotional material out to customers.

- **Use note cards.** Keep small note cards on regular guests so that everyone in the restaurant is familiar with their likes and dislikes, table preferences and any other pertinent information that will enable you to treat them like royalty. Try rewarding your staff for increasing the note card collection and for reaching a specific number each month.

- **Create club memberships.** Extend extra privileges and restaurant paraphernalia that is exclusive to members. For example, introduce unique items, such as mugs or glasses. Make them different in either color or design. Engrave customer names on them. Or, maybe, provide free T-shirts, hats or other items that they can wear and advertise your restaurant. Consider offering these items based on how many specific items they might have ordered over a period of time, such as oysters, barbecue ribs or some other specialty item.

- **Follow-up contact.** Thank customers for choosing your restaurant. A personal handwritten postcard makes an even better impression.

- **Fax a thank you.** After a large business group dines at your restaurant, send them a thank-you fax at the office. Tell them you enjoyed serving them and hope to see them again soon.

- **Send celebration cards.** Once you've acquired a list of personal information, you're in a position to send customers anniversary and birthday cards.

Actions That Grab Attention

There are several small actions you can take that will grab the attention of potential guests passing by your restaurant. Don't ignore simple free marketing techniques that have worked for decades. Here are some tips:

- **Use window displays.** A sign in the window works well, but a moving object in the window is so much more effective. For instance, The Rainforest Café is built and decorated around a nature-theme, amusement park design. How about a dancing gorilla in the window?

- **Use chimes.** Signs have to be seen to be recognized. Use chimes at the entrance of your building. They sing to customers who aren't paying attention in a way that signs do not.

- **Use large, distinctive glassware.** For special drinks use large, distinctive glassware. Make guests turn their heads and take notice as your staff passes by carrying those unique beverages.

- **Menu highlighting.** Simple, but effective. Use boldface, italic or a different color. You could also use callout words such as "special," "new," "traditional" or "tasty" beside the item.

The "Do Nots" of a Profitable Business

You may have a foolproof business plan, with projected profits that look extremely encouraging – on paper! But it's often the little practicalities that let you down and reduce your profits without you realizing it:

- **Don't offer regular discounts.** Discounts and coupons are great for drawing customers on a short-term basis, but they don't buy customer loyalty and can actually hurt you in the long run.

- **Don't provide discounts to existing customers.** Providing discounts to existing customers doesn't benefit you. Instead, buy an occasional drink or dessert.

Maximize Wine Sales

Wine sales produce high profit margins. Here are some tips to help you make the most of wine sales:

- **Opening wine.** Ensure that your employees are skilled at opening a bottle of wine and that they feel comfortable before sending them out to test their skills on your customers.

- **Pronouncing the wine list.** Your staff should know how to pronounce each wine on the wine list. Take time to cover this issue during training. Remember, the more they know, the more they can sell to your customers.

- **Pronunciation isn't enough.** Once your staff has the pronunciation of each wine down pat, they also need to know which wines go with which foods and desserts.

- **Anticipate questions.** During the staff briefing, run over commonly asked questions regarding the wine menu. Also, anticipate questions that guests are most likely to ask. Don't allow your staff to be caught off guard. Give them ideas on exactly how to phrase specific answers.

- **Wine sells itself, or does it?** Offer customers a taste of different wines. Wine can't sell itself, until you sell the idea of trying it.

- **Offer limited taste tests.** Depending on your local laws, offer two to three taste-test samples when guests are trying to decide upon a particular wine. This is not only courteous and convenient to your patrons, but it also gives the wine a chance to sell itself. Consider pairing a particular glass of wine with each course of food on the menu.

- **Display wine cases.** Display wines in the lobby, lounge or dining room. If guests are waiting to be seated, they can browse your selection of wines before they even see a menu.

- **Use wine descriptions.** Provide more taste information on your wine list. Today's guests are often very sophisticated wine drinkers. They want the exact low-down on the wines they have so carefully selected to accompany their meals.

- **Include wine on the dessert menu.** Add a selection of wines to your dessert menu that satisfies the sweet tooth. Some of these wines could be great alternatives for guests who prefer not to order dessert, or serve as a great combination with specific desserts. Consider including after-dinner wines to the overall selection as well.

- **Wine by the bottle, half bottle or glass.** Offer wine selections by the bottle and the glass. That way, those who might not want a whole bottle have the option of ordering only half a bottle or a simple glass. List prices on the menu for each serving size of wine. This eliminates confusion and greatly improves communication.

Manage Costs – Increase Sales

Managing business costs such as inventory, supplies, labor and other services takes focus and consistency. But, there are also a few easy tips that can help you keep such costs to a minimum. Utilize existing resources, such as:

- **Expand sales without additional investment.** Provide a display case selling specialty items that

can last for a few days or even weeks. Have your
chef prepare these items during the slow hours.
Many guests would love the idea of purchasing
items "to go" that they can't purchase in a store or
anywhere else. Utilize existing resources and
create additional sales on the side.

- **Virgin drinks.** Offer a wide selection of virgin
  specialty drinks for children, non-drinkers and
  designated drivers. This saves you the expense of
  providing free refills on coffee, tea and sodas.

- **Sell water.** Offer customers a choice of bottled
  water such as spring water, still water, sparkling
  water or even flavored water, before you simply
  pour them a glass of ice water from a pitcher.
  You'll be amazed at how much this simple act will
  increase your sales figures.

- **Reduce waste.** Remove all garbage cans from the
  kitchen and instead place plastic tubs throughout
  the prep area. This way, at the end of each shift,
  the tubs' contents can be checked to ensure the
  proper procedures are being followed for
  preparation and trimming raw products. Make
  workers accountable for the quality of their work.

Other Cost-Saving Tips

You may well have trimmed your inventory and
staffing costs, but in a restaurant environment,
many other possibilities exist for cost control. Consider
the following opportunities:

- **Lease icemakers.** Icemakers are costly to
  purchase and repair. Rent or lease icemakers on

an as-needed basis instead. However, if you already have an icemaker, be sure to install appropriate filters in the unit to enable it to last longer. Contact the following companies for leasing restaurant equipment and supplies:

- Arctic Refrigeration & Equipment, www.arctic-foodequip.com, 866-528-8528

- Easy Lease Company, www.easyleasecompany.com, 800-514-4047

- Global Restaurant Equipment & Supplies, www.globalrestaurantequip.com, 800-666-8099

- National Leasing Network, www.oraclewiz.com/restaurant_equipment_leas ing.htm, 520-682-7124

- **Install electric hand dryers.** Not only do they save on costs, they are also better for sanitation purposes. Contact:
  - ASI Electric Dryer, www.cescompany.com, 707-664-9964

  - Stielbel Eltron, www.stiebel-eltron-usa.com, 800-582-8423

  - World Dryer, www.worlddryer.com, 800-323-0701

- **Return pallets and crates to vendors.** Pallets and crates take up valuable space, as they are bulky items requiring labor to manage them. By making vendors responsible for taking pallets away and reusing them, the burden on your staff is reduced as well as the costs of waste management.

- **Save on table-top items.** To eliminate the use of individual wrapping, use straw and toothpick dispensers. Also, consider using drink coasters that can be reused instead of cocktail napkins. Decorations do not have to be expensive. Consider browsing through online party and decoration sites:
  - 123 Party, www.123party.com

  - D & D Design, www.ddchili.com

  - General Plastics Corporation, www.genplast.com, 800-888-3833

  - Grab A Bargain, www.grababargain.com

  - Irvin's Tinware Company, www.irvintinware.com, 570-539-8200

  - Island Madness, www.islandmadness.com/cocktail1html

  - Party Cheap, www.partycheap.com, 800-224-3143.

- **Offer discounts for mugs.** Offer discounts to customers who bring in reusable mugs for refills. Several restaurants have similar programs that encourage customers to reduce unnecessary waste. The incentive to bring in their own mug works when they receive beverages at reduced prices. Contact:
  - Advertising Magic, www.advertisingmagic.com, 800-862-4421

  - Ceramic Mugs,www.ceramic-mugs.com, 305-593-0911

- DADEC Photo Mugs & Gifts, www.dadec.com, 866-853-3257

- Gift Mugs, www.giftmugs.com, 321-253-0012

- My Promo Store, www.mypromostore.com, 877-838-3700

- **Use cleaning rags instead of paper towels.** Encourage staff to use cleaning rags instead of high-quality napkins and paper towels to mop up a spill. The purchase of disposable towels and napkins can be more expensive than laundry service.

- **Install thermal strips over cooler and freezer doors.** Keep cold air in and warm air out. This increases efficiency and reduces unnecessary electricity usage so that the compressor doesn't have to work as hard. Here are a few companies that provide seal-tight doors and replacement parts:
  - Arrow Restaurant Equipment, www.arrowreste.com, 909-621-7428

  - Commercial Appliance, www.commappl.com, 800-481-7373

  - Loadmaster, www.loadmaster.com, 514-636-1243

  - **Separate hot and cold appliances.** Separate the locations of hot and cold appliances. It will increase efficiency and temperature regulation. Draw out an organizational diagram of your kitchen. The one-time effort will be worth it.

CHAPTER TEN

BEHIND THE SCENES

Managing the Flow in the Kitchen

Organization in the kitchen is essential for smooth operations and guest satisfaction. Schedule conflicts, lack of resources, cramped spaces and overworked employees can create daily havoc. A clean, organized kitchen allows for better functionality. The following are tips that will help you avoid chaos in the kitchen:

- **Chefs.** Chefs need to face the kitchen entrance so that they can have an overall view of who's entering and who's leaving. It's easier for them to direct order and flow if they can see what's going on without stopping their own work.

- **Working with tight kitchen space.** If you have only a small amount of space to work with in the kitchen, then add a large mirror on the wall. This way the chef can look up to see what's going on behind and around him. It also reflects space, giving the impression of more space than there actually is available. The following are a few companies where you may order large or customized mirrors:
  - Advanced Optics, www.advancedoptics.com, 515-964-5050

  - City Glass and Mirror Inc., www.cityglassand-mirror.com, 866-831-7100

- Genessee Glass & Mirror, www.wefixglass.com 585-621-3580

- Mesko Glass, www.mesko.com, 800-982-4055

- See All, www.seeall.com, 773-927-3232

- **Hanging notices and reminders in the kitchen.** The kitchen is a difficult place to post items, as heat and steam tend to wrinkle papers and affect the durability of adhesives.

- **Laminate recipe cards.** Print up recipe cards and have them laminated. This will help them to last longer. Keep them in an easily accessible area in the kitchen and require all staff to follow your recipes for all meals. Do the same thing in the bar area. Like food, mixed drinks should be prepared the same way every time. Make sure that customers can know what to expect when they place an order.

- **Use preventative maintenance.** Instruct your staff on the importance of performing preventative maintenance on all kitchen appliances and equipment in order to achieve the best possible efficiency. Schedule individual personnel to perform preventative maintenance, as needed, so that they rotate the responsibility. Keep the care instructions that came with the package. Have them typed, laminated and hung above the appliance or placed with it in storage.

Safety in the Restaurant

Enforcing safety throughout your restaurant for both guests and employees, can lower your workers' compensation costs and your business insurance. Here are a few safety tips:

- **Tell them it's hot!** Make sure your customers realize the plates are hot. Obvious, but also necessary – remind them that their coffee is hot. Your simple warning can prevent them from burning their tongue, a child from burning a finger or an adult from sipping coffee that is too hot to taste.

- **Safe booster seats and high chairs.** Use steady and stable booster seats and high chairs that have a mechanism for buckling a belt around the child's waist for additional safety measures. Many booster seats don't have a belt, which allow a child to slide down and easily slip beneath the table. This is a safety hazard and should not be tolerated in your restaurant. The following online companies sell high chairs and booster seats for restaurants:
  - High Chair World, www.highchairworld.com, 800-821-9153

  - Net Kids Wear, www.netkidswear.com, 732-203-9677

  - Old Dominion Wood Products, www.yah-wehsaliveandwell.com, 386-437-1100

  - Restaurant Equipment, www.restaurantequipment.com, 800-845-6677

Kitchen Safety

Although safety standards are an operational priority throughout your establishment, the kitchen is the highest risk area of all and requires constant attention. Remain alert, at all times, to the following hazards:

- **Use no-cut gloves.** Establish a rule that anyone using a knife must wear no-cut gloves. When moving from food product to product, have your employees wear rubber gloves over the no-cut glove to prevent cross-contamination. An online site that provides no-cut gloves is www.atlantic-pub.com.

- **Slip-resistant shoes.** Require all your employees to wear shoes with slip-resistant soles. Studies have shown that this preventative measure greatly reduces the risk of falls, resulting in less on-the-job injury claims. Check out online shoes sites such as:
  - Lehigh Safety Shoes, www.lehighsafety.com, 800-444-4086

  - Nautilus Footwear, www.nautilusfootwear.com, 888-269-4526

  - Shoes for Crews, www.shoesforcrews.com, 800-329-0102

- **Clean sponges.** Replace or clean sponges after every use. Dirty sponges are a haven for bacteria. The best way to clean a sponge is to toss it into the dishwasher with your next load. Remember that detergent and high temperatures help keep harmful bacteria away.

- **Hats and gloves.** Require and provide appropriate hats and gloves for kitchen staff handling food preparation and cooking. This is for their own safety as well as that of the guests eating the food.

- **Prevent burns in the kitchen.** Ensure that potholders are dry. Wet potholders produce steam, which can be even hotter than boiling water. Never lift a pot or a pan without using a potholder. Have potholders available at every cooking station in the kitchen and require all chefs and assistants to use them.

- **Cooking with hot oil.** Be very careful when adding food to hot oil. Protect your eyes from hot splatters that can be damaging. Wear protective glasses and/or turn your head before you toss in the food.

- **Install a fireproof wall behind the hood.** Never tolerate wood or any kind of cover that can easily burn. Make sure you have a firewall behind the hood. The more fireproof your kitchen, the better your possibilities of stopping potential fires before they rage out of control.

General Safety Factors

Safety should be a priority, in all areas of your operation, not just the kitchen and restaurant. Safety is as much of a concern outside your restaurant as inside:

- **Parking lot.** Make sure that your parking lot is well lit. Check for burned-out lights. Replace them immediately. Provide clear signs and directions.

Highlight handicapped parking places. In winter weather, ensure that your parking lot is properly scraped and salted.

- **Fire drills.** Most fires are small kitchen fires that can be put out quickly if handled appropriately. Ensure that every employee knows where the fire extinguishers are located. Have fire drills where employees are trained how to use fire extinguishers.

- **Evacuation procedures.** Have a safety plan in place that clearly defines how employees are to handle customers in the event of an emergency. Also, escape routes should be clearly marked.

- **Install a window in the back door.** Install a window so you can see exactly who is at the door before opening it. Typically, vendors arrive at your back door for deliveries. Question anyone who isn't driving a delivery truck or that you don't recognize. If in doubt, don't open the door. Put up a sign outside the back door requiring visitors to show ID.

- **No overloading.** Never allow employees to overload carts, rolling racks or the hot boxes. This is very dangerous and could cause severe injury.

Create a Food Safety – HACCP Plan

One food poisoning outbreak case could cost your restaurant's reputation and your entire business. Don't let it happen to you. Develop an effective food-safety plan – HACCP (Hazardous Area Critical Control Points) that identifies where potential food contamination and hazards could occur. Here are some essential guidelines:

- **Devise a food-safety plan that covers the following issues:**
  - Selecting appropriate suppliers and documenting specific arrangements with them.

  - How to handle a product recall being issued by the manufacturer.

  - Personal hygiene.

  - Cross-contamination and safety guidelines.

  - Cleaning and washing procedures. Include equipment, food and employees' hands, etc.

  - Safe cooking procedures. Include details about correct temperatures.

  - Handling a customer with food poisoning.

- **Produce written copies of food safety procedures.** Give a copy to each member of staff. Also laminate a copy and post it in a strategic position in the kitchen.

- **Use separate utensils for raw and cooked food.** Never mix the same utensils used for uncooked food with cooked food. Use separate color-coded cutting boards, utensils and brushes for cooked and uncooked food. Wash and sanitize surface areas immediately after preparing food. Color-coded cutting boards may be found at www.atlantic-pub.com.

- **Use non-metallic containers.** Ingredients used in marinades, such as wine, vinegar and lemon juice, are acidic and can cause a chemical reaction with certain metals. When this happens, the food can be adversely affected.

- **Boil marinade sauces.** If you plan to use a marinade sauce that has come into contact with raw meat, do not use it with cooked food until you bring it to a boil for at least a whole minute. Otherwise, mix the marinade sauce and separate it into two different bowls.

- **Serving buffet food.** Keep cold food on ice at a temperature below 40° F. Keep hot food at an internal temperature of at least 140° F. When replenishing a buffet, do not mix fresh food with food that has already been set out to serve.

- **A few Web sites with more food safety related information are:**
  - Atlantic Publishing, www.atlantic-pub.com

  - Food and Nutrition Information Center, www.nal.usda.gov/fnic

  - CDC Food Safety Office, www.cdc.gov/foodsafety

  - National Food Processors Association (NFPA), www.nfpa-food.org

  - The Food Safety Consortium, www.uark.edu/depts/fsc/othersites.html

The Power of Purchasing - Be an Astute Buyer

Restaurant owners and managers that can bring their costs down to the absolute minimum, while maintaining standards and quality, will succeed in today's restaurant trade. Try the following tips:

- **Develop multiple vendor relationships.** Ideally, have at least one major vendor for each food category and then a backup supplier from whom you purchase occasionally. This is good for continued competition.

- **Know the price cycles.** Some frozen vegetables and other foods have an annual price cycle, while other fruits, vegetables and grains have prices that vary according to their harvest season. Animal proteins have price cycles that vary according to slaughter peaks during the calendar year. Be aware of these cycles and time your purchase activity to take advantage of the best prices available.

- **Utilize fixed prices.** If you anticipate rising prices on a particular product, consider a fixed price agreement for a specific period of time, regardless of the market fluctuations. Fixed prices are more appropriate for purchasing frozen, canned or dried food items.

- **Market price date-of-shipment.** Use this purchasing method for fresh food items where the guaranteed supply of freshness is more important than the actual price. This means that the prices are flexible and subject to change at any given notice. Therefore, buyers pay the going market rate on the actual date that the item is shipped.

- **Purchasing cleaning supplies.** Request your vendor to supply several samples of various cleaning supplies. This gives you a chance to determine which brands work best for you.

- **Use specifications to buy meat.** Take advantage of government specifications and guidelines as well as those of nationwide organizations. These specifications have been designed and tested over a period of years for the safety and health of everyone. Go to the following Web sites for more information on meat specifications:
  - North American Meat Processors Association (NAMP), www.namp.com

  - American Association of Meat Processors (AAMP), www.aamp.com

  - American Meat Institute (AMI), www.meatami.com

Develop a Buying Plan

Based on the research you've done regarding vendors and pricing, as well as harvest and slaughter schedules, begin listing the foods you'll need and the quantity you plan to purchase for each month, beginning in January:

- **Write down all the foods and ingredients** you'll need to purchase throughout the year.

- **List items in categories.**

- **Separate the foods that need to be purchased fresh** as opposed to frozen, canned or processed foods.

- **Create a different list for all non-food purchases**, such as table-top items and cleaning supplies.

INDEX

U

Uniform System of
Accounts for Restaurants,
   19
uniforms, 113
unique selling position,
   116
usable Trim, 42
utilities, 9

W

wages, 9
waste, 42
Web site, 117
window displays, 123
wine sales, 124
working capital, 37

Y

yield, 42
yield costs, 41